M000284792

"Dr. Randy Clark has been a dear friend for many years. He is passionate to know God and make Him known. Randy wants to be a catalyst to draw many others into deeper relationship with God. I pray this book will be a resource to grow your faith and increase your hunger for God as you read these powerful testimonies!"

—HEIDI G. BAKER, PhD,
cofounder and CEO of Iris Global

"This is such a wonderful book! Randy Clark writes, 'The Christian life was never meant to be boring.' He then goes on to prove it. With an academic's eye for evidence and logical argument, he dismantles the circular reasoning of those skeptical about the miraculous while—at the same time—empirically proving the reality of God's supernatural power on the earth. *Eyewitness to Miracles* is written in an open (nondenominational) way, challenging believers to actively press into the supernatural and challenging the church to do a better job at verifying and recording supernatural healings. Ultimately, this book carries an exciting charge to believers—to live in the fullness of God's transformative power, so that we can partner with Him in bringing heaven to earth."

—BILL JOHNSON, Bethel Church, Redding, CA;
author of *When Heaven Invades Earth* and *God Is Good*

"All I can say is *finally*! I have been waiting my whole life for a book like this so I can share a credible perspective on the actual fruit of healing ministry. This is such a well-crafted document, and it will give people who have a believing but skeptical nature permission to finally believe what they suspected: God is a healer and healing can be proven! I believe churches, individuals, and doctors will all find it a refreshing prototype on how to report and build faith through true stories. Randy Clark is leading the body of Christ into credibility when it comes to healing ministry, and these stories don't just cause an emotional reaction; they build a spiritual momentum."

—SHAWN BOLZ, author, television host,
producer, and minister

"Once in a while a book comes along that you wish you could put into the hands of everyone, believer and doubter! On June 6, 1995, Randy Clark was used by God to give me, a conservative Baptist pastor, an upgrade that forever changed my life and ministry. I became an eyewitness to miracles, signs, and wonders, and since that time we have seen more than a million names added to the Lamb's Book of Life. Randy is a scholar and storyteller; his book is filled with the passion of a man who has pursued Jesus with his whole self! This book is explosive and his personal experiences will open your eyes to seeing the hand of God moving in the Western world."

—LEIF HETLAND, president,
Global Mission Awareness

EYEWITNESS TO
MIRACLES

EYEWITNESS TO
MIRACLES

WATCHING THE GOSPEL
COME TO LIFE

RANDY CLARK

EMANATE
BOOKS

Published in Nashville, Tennessee, by Emanate Books, an imprint of Thomas Nelson. Emanate Books and Thomas Nelson are registered trademarks of HarperCollins Christian Publishing, Inc.

Thomas Nelson titles may be purchased in bulk for educational, business, fund-raising, or sales promotional use. For information, please e-mail SpecialMarkets@ThomasNelson.com.

ISBN: 9780785219125 (eBook)

ISBN: 9780785219057 (TP)

Library of Congress Control Number: 2017956812

Printed in the United States of America

18 19 20 21 22   LSC   10 9 8 7 6 5 4 3 2 1

CONTENTS

I want to dedicate this book to the people who helped me as mentors, advisors, and professional associates with my doctor of ministry thesis. You helped increase my hunger to learn and to defend the faith once and for all delivered to the saints. A faith that is not limited to doctrinal or creedal confessions but is also about the faith that advances the kingdom of God through signs and wonders, miracles and healings.

Andrew Sung Park, PhD, professor of theology and ethics at United Theological Seminary, faculty advisor/mentor

Jon Ruthven, PhD, professor emeritus, Regent University School of Divinity, faculty mentor

Gary Greig, PhD, former assistant professor of Old Testament at Regent Divinity School, faculty mentor

Martin Moore-Ede, MD, PhD, former professor of medicine, Harvard Medical School, professional advisor

Stephen Mory, MD, PhD, psychiatrist, professional advisor

John Park, MD, specializing in pain treatment, professional advisor

Mary Healey, PhD, associate professor of Scripture at Sacred Heart Major Seminary, Roman Catholic advisor

Craig Keener, PhD, professor of New Testament at Asbury Theological Seminary, New Testament advisor

Candace Brown, PhD, professor of religious studies, Indiana University, medical studies advisor

Joshua Brown, PhD, professor of psychological and brain sciences, Indiana University, medical studies advisor

Michael McClymond, PhD, professor of modern Christianity, Saint Louis University, historical theology advisor

FOREWORD

As a professor in the sciences at a large research university, I take a fairly critical view toward claims of scientific evidence. In science, the state of knowledge advances through critical inquiry, well-designed studies, and rigorous analysis. Over a decade ago, early in my career, I faced a personal health crisis in which I expected to die within a short period of time despite the best medical treatment. That experience, as it played out over about a year, motivated me to examine claims of nonmedical healing. I wanted to see firsthand what people experienced, and being the skeptical scientist that I am, I wanted to see what evidence there was, if any, that healings happened apart from medical intervention. My intention was to pick apart the experiences and evidence to see what could withstand critical scrutiny, for as much as I wanted healing for myself, I did not want to waste time entertaining grand claims devoid of evidence.

What I found first seemed to confirm my suspicions—for the most part, the Pentecostal and charismatic Christians who reported healing through prayer seemed to care relatively little about evidence. They were content simply to testify about their healing experiences to an audience of the faithful, who required no proof. This bothered me. I noticed that leaders in other religious traditions were quite willing to have their practices and their effects examined with scientific methods, and admirably so in my opinion. No less than the Dalai Lama has made a point of reaching out to neuroscientists to study Buddhist mindfulness meditation and its effects on the brain. In my research field of cognitive neuroscience, a number of my academic colleagues have reported interesting results from their studies of Buddhist monks and mindfulness meditation. This in turn has greatly enhanced the influence of such practices on Western culture. Why, I wondered, did Christian communities place so little value on careful investigation and evidence of their own practices and claims?

It was against this backdrop that I first met Randy Clark in a large meeting in which he was a featured speaker. I was struck by how approachable he was, and in subsequent conversations, I was struck even more by how much he cared about research and evidence as it relates to prayer for healing. At the same time, my wife, Candy Gunther Brown, also began studying healing claims in her capacity as a professor of religious studies at a large research university. Randy Clark was instrumental in helping our research team get access to a number of populations where healing claims were common, especially with Heidi Baker in Mozambique and others in Brazil, Canada, and the United States. Out of that came a number of scholarly research works, including my wife's book *Testing Prayer* (Harvard University Press) and her article assessing hearing and vision improvement following healing prayer, published in the peer-reviewed *Southern Medical Journal*. This helped define a field of scholarly inquiry on proximal intercessory prayer.

After the initial round of research, Randy Clark, my wife and I, and other PhD and MD academics and medical researchers began to consider how we could scale up the research and bring critical inquiry to more healing prayer claims. Out of that we formed GMRI, the Global Medical Research Institute (globalmri.org), a 501(c)(3) non-profit organization with the mission of bringing rigorous biomedical investigation and critical inquiry to Christian healing prayer practices.

GMRI examines individual cases and controlled trials. For individual case reports, we look at medical records of individuals before and after claimed healings. We preserve their anonymity, and we consider all the possible ways their medical records could be explained. In some cases, we have found plausible medical explanations of claimed healings, but in others, our medical experts have found no plausible explanation, given the current state of medical knowledge. For controlled trials, we look at groups of individuals, asking whether particular faith practices and experiences are associated with different health outcomes on average. I am grateful for Randy Clark's enthusiasm for studying healing experiences and rigorously examining all available evidence, wherever it may lead. It is my hope that the value he places on medical evidence will inspire others in his community to likewise value evidence and scientific inquiry into healing claims. I believe this would be good for everyone, believers and skeptics alike.

In what follows, Randy Clark provides an excellent front-row seat for healing prayer practices and experiences, of which he has seen countless and often dramatic examples over the years. These are the kinds of claims that are both inspiring on a human level and a rich source of primary-source ethnographic research materials on an academic level. I, for one, am grateful to many Christians, Randy Clark among them, who prayed for my healing. Today, I am alive and well, despite an initially poor medical prognosis and the unavailability of any curative medical treatment. Randy Clark brings a unique perspective, weaving his extensive experience together with a historical review and his own theological perspectives. To his credit, he does not shy away from considering a number of explanations of the phenomena he observes, such as placebo effects. His dissertation work on individuals with surgically implanted metal, as summarized in this book, represents a bold attempt to explore new frontiers in spiritual healing claims. The findings invite follow-up to investigate individual cases for medical evidence as well as controlled studies that would allow population-level inferences. I hope this book will help to inspire such inquiry.

JOSHUA BROWN, PHD
Professor of Psychological and Brain Sciences
Indiana University

• • •

As a professor of religious studies, I have spent the past fifteen years studying spiritual healing practices. Observing the exponential growth of global Pentecostal and charismatic Christianity, I asked what accounts for this growth. My research pointed to the unparalleled significance of divine healing and deliverance practices. Many people worldwide are attracted to Pentecostalism because they need—and seem to experience—nonmedical healing. There are many possible explanations for such experiences. I have examined both medical and nonmedical interpretations. My research encompasses comparison of medical records from before and after healing experiences; surveys of prayer practitioners; clinical trials; and multiyear follow-up.

Conducting empirical research on prayer for healing requires cooperation from practitioners, ideally including leaders of large and influential ministries. Such cooperation is not always easy to obtain. Many Pentecostal leaders and members are hesitant to allow access to professional researchers for various reasons: they may not see the value of medical investigation, they may worry that medical scrutiny will undermine faith, or they may fear media scandals or lawsuits.

I first met Randy Clark in 2003. I approached him, alongside numerous other Pentecostal leaders, requesting permission to distribute a survey to participants in meetings where prayer was offered for healing. Whereas other Pentecostal leaders either refused my similar requests outright or nominally agreed but failed to follow through, Randy Clark actually seemed to welcome scholarly investigation. He encouraged meeting attendees to take the time to fill out my surveys and give me copies of their medical records from before and after healing prayer experiences. He also introduced me to other influential ministry leaders and urged them to cooperate with me, despite their hesitations. Without Randy Clark's help, I simply could not have done the research that resulted in a "Study of the Therapeutic Effects of Proximal Intercessory Prayer (STEPP) on Auditory and Visual Impairments in Rural Mozambique," *Southern Medical Journal* (2010); and *Testing Prayer: Science and Healing* (Harvard University Press, 2012).

In addition to welcoming research by outside investigators, Randy Clark is also exceptionally interested in bringing a medical lens to bear on the healing phenomena that are so frequently reported in his meetings. This interest stirred him to write a doctoral dissertation investigating the long-term effects of healing experiences on individuals with documented medical conditions that had required metal to be surgically implanted. This is a pioneering effort that should be welcomed by prayer practitioners, medical doctors, scholars, and policy makers for what it can reveal about the effects of prayer practices.

More such serious investigation is needed if religious and secular leaders are to cut through the abundance of confusion and controversy that continues to surround healing prayer practices. The paucity of such research motivated the founding of the Global Medical Research Institute. GMRI's mission is to facilitate review of medical records from before and after remarkable healing prayer experiences by a panel of medical specialists; to publish case reports of medically unexplained healing experiences; and to support rigorous clinical studies.

Randy Clark's example illustrates that much of the mutual

suspicion that divides practitioners of healing prayer from those who study it is unnecessary and indeed unhelpful. All interested parties stand to benefit from learning more about what happens when people pray for healing.

CANDY GUNTHER BROWN, PHD

Professor of Religious Studies, Indiana University

Author of *Testing Prayer: Science and Healing and The Healing Gods: Complementary and Alternative Medicine in Christian America*

INTRODUCTION

Not all introductions are at the beginning of a relationship. Sometimes one is only introduced formally to the person he or she has already been speaking with hours later. I want you to meet the story before I officially introduce you to the cast. The introductions to the doctoral thesis and the doctoral advisors and seminary mentors, along with an introduction to the ministry of Global Awakening, where most of the stories occurred, and an introduction to me are at the end of the book. The choice is yours: you can have your introduction before you read, during the reading, or after you have completed *Eyewitness to Miracles*. The only introduction I have placed here is the introduction to the structure of the book and its purpose.

There are two parts to *Eyewitness to Miracles*. The first part is composed of testimonies, the vast majority of which I witnessed. These testimonies deal with miracles and the supernatural. Part 1 consists of five chapters.

This work begins with evidence for the miraculous. People often say, "I will believe it when I see it." It is this desire to show the miraculous with which we begin. In addition, to the videos of the testimonies of healings and miracles already mentioned, I also cover my personal experience with angels and the spiritual realm while on my international ministry trips. I then discuss out-of-body experiences. Some stories are about people who died and came back to life (dead raisings), others about people who were taken to heaven without having died, and other near-death experiences. I cover a story of bilocation as well. Further, I discuss hearing the audible voice of God. I share about *xenolalia*, the ability to speak a language, or languages, supernaturally, without learning the language. Finally, I describe numerous physical healings, including the healing of people with bipolar disorder or schizophrenia, quadriplegics and paraplegics, blind persons, deaf persons, and so on. I also talk about people healed of Parkinson's, cancer, MS, and amputations, as well as how certain people were healed by holy laughter.

Part 2, which consists of ten chapters, is about the problems related to miracles. I deal with skeptics, their definition of miracles, and their resultant arguments against miracles, as well as how they attempt to explain them away. I will touch on how they use a circular argument that makes it impossible to prove miracles by their logic. In addition, I lay out the biblical definition of what is referred to as miracles today, and it presents the arguments for miracles. I also consider the difference between two conservative worldviews regarding miracles and compare their positions in light of the Bible. I include an analysis of the biblical passages that use different words for the demonstrations of the power of God that include the concept of miracle though the word *miracle* itself may not be used. I analyze three different worldviews held by biblical scholars that impact their understanding of miracles both in biblical times and today. Finally, I review opportunities to grow in the supernatural realm of ministries, a "Now that I believe, what is the next step?" approach.

Now let us begin with evidence for miracles—actual visual evidence—evidence you can see.

TESTIMONIES ON VIDEO

Many of the individuals healed in the following stories consented to sharing their testimonies right after their healings occurred. These testimonies were captured on video and are available for you to view online at: globalawakening.com/eyewitnesstomiracles. This URL can also be found in the endnotes that reference healing testimonies. It is one thing to read a story; it is another to see someone telling about it right after his or her healing. These videos make this book all the more believable and endearing. For each such story, just type the above URL into your browser and search. And for those with even greater interest in the subject, hundreds more healings can be watched on YouTube.com. Search for the Global Awakening YouTube Channel, which has a global logo of a man falling back into earth. Under "Playlists," select Notable Testimonies to view many healing testimonies, and many more to come.

PART ONE

THE EVIDENCE FOR THE MIRACULOUS

The blind receive sight, the lame walk, those who have leprosy are cleansed, the deaf hear, the dead are raised, and the good news is proclaimed to the poor.

—LUKE 7:22

CHAPTER 1

THE BLIND SEE

I n this chapter we will look at the amazing testimonies of those who were once blind, but now see. We begin with a story from Brazil.

MAN'S EYEBALL HEALED
IN SOUTHERN BRAZIL

In Brazil, a young man's eyeball was healed by prayer. According to the man's mother, he had not seen anything but a black spot out of his left eye from the time he was a baby. He had only 5 percent vision in that eye, and that was blurry and cloudy. But after someone prayed for him, the young man said he could see. His mother confirmed that her son had never been able to see numbers, but once he was healed, he was able to call out every number he was shown.

• • •

In addition to that remarkable story, the following stories reveal that God is still in the business of giving sight to the blind.

MAN HEALED FROM BLINDNESS IN LEFT EYE

In Forteleza, Brazil, a man blind from birth was healed and able to see. In an update with a pastor and church-growth expert, we learned that the man had been born without the optic nerve attached to the back of his eye. A creative miracle occurred, and his optic nerve grew in where there had previously not been one.[1]

BELFAST, IRELAND, WOMAN READS AGAIN

During the last fifteen years, I have seen hundreds of blind eyes opened, and many who were blind in both eyes healed. The preponderance of these healings occurred in Brazil, though others were in India, Cambodia, Argentina, Ireland, Guatemala, and several other countries, including the United States. The first person healed of blindness when I prayed was a woman in Northern Ireland. I remember her to this day. She was in her home and told my associate, Mark Endres, and me that she missed being able to read the Bible. Diabetes had destroyed her eyes, and she could no longer see. We prayed, and God restored her sight.

ARGENTINE WOMAN RECEIVES SIGHT

A few weeks later, Kirk Hintz, a friend from my church in St. Louis, was with me in Argentina. There were eleven of us on this trip. It was my first time bringing a team with me to minister. Kirk was getting ready to go to sleep in our hotel room when he said, "Now I realize just how skeptical we are in North America. I am sitting here thinking about what I saw with my own eyes, and I am struggling to believe my own eyes. I prayed for a woman tonight who was deaf in her left ear and blind in her left eye. Her eye was white instead of brown. The second time I prayed for her, she opened her eye and it was normal, the white had turned back to brown, and she could see." I have never forgotten Kirk's head-on collision with his Western skepticism.

WOMAN BLIND FROM DIABETES
SEES HER HUSBAND'S FACE

The next night I was praying for a woman who had neuropathy and colon problems. God healed her, for which she was very happy. When she started to leave, she told me that she was also blind due to her long battle with diabetes. Having just prayed a few weeks earlier in Northern Ireland for diabetes-induced blindness, I was excited to see my second diabetic blind person be healed. She was hesitant, not wanting to be prayed for, thankful enough that she had been healed of her severe abdominal pain. I told her about the woman who had just been healed of blindness from diabetes a few weeks before, and asked her to let me pray for her. She consented.

I prayed several times for her as she gradually began to receive her sight. At first she could see only the brightness of a large, bright light over us. With more prayer, she could see objects but couldn't tell that they were people. After we prayed again, she could see what she knew were people, but they were very blurry, and she couldn't see color yet. Then I felt the Lord impress me to tell her that I was going to pray for her one more time, and after this time she would be able to see clearly.

I began to pray for her, and as I was praying, I had her husband, who had also been blind, come stand about four feet in front of her. When I finished praying, I stepped out of her line of sight. She saw and recognized her husband, and they fell into each other's arms, weeping with gratitude for the ability to see each other again. These were the first two blind people who were healed under my ministry. You never forget your firsts.

SIX BLIND PEOPLE HEALED IN
ONE NIGHT IN BRAZIL

The most blind eyes and blind people I saw healed in one night happened in Goiania, a bustling city of more than one million people in southern Brazil. I was at the Videra Church, a highly educated church that had grown from three thousand the first time I visited to about thirty thousand average attendance. Once again I had a Global Awakening International Ministry team with me of about seventy people. The pastor, Aloisio Silva, had never seen a blind person healed until that night. There was a strong anointing for the blind. He prayed for two who were healed of blindness. There were four more blind people healed that night.

I prayed for one of the blind persons healed that night, a woman who was totally blind. During the interview to find out what might be the cause of the blindness, helping me pray more specifically, I discovered nothing to indicate it might not be blindness from a natural cause. I prayed several times, but there was no improvement. Each time I reinterviewed her to see if she could see any better, her answer was no.

Then I had an impression to ask her specifically when she went blind. What was going on at the time? Was there anything traumatic that occurred before her onset of blindness?

She responded, "The only traumatic event was the death of my father."

"How close was the onset of blindness to your father's death?" I asked.

"Immediately."

I probed further. "Were you with your father when he died?"

"Yes," she said.

Finally, I asked her, "Were you touching your father when he died?"

"Yes."

Suddenly, I felt I knew why she was blind. It was not due to a natural cause; neither was it due to the psychological trauma of her father's death. I believed it was caused by an afflicting spirit that had been in her father and that had entered her at the time of his death.

I told her, "I am going to pray for you one more time, and after this prayer you will be able to see."

This is what I call a gift of faith. I do not say that to people in order to build their faith. There had been no improvement up to this point. I prayed, "I command this afflicting spirit to leave this woman, and I command her eyes to see. Eyes, in the name of Jesus, I command you to see. I command this spirit of affliction to leave in Jesus' name."

Then I told her to open her eyes. When she did, she could see. We were all so excited to witness the blind see that night, and to discover the authority we have in Jesus' name.

THE GREATEST MIRACLE IN GOIÂNIA

On that same night there was a man who was not healed of his blindness, which he'd had for more than fifty years. Six were healed, but he wasn't. This was a very unusual story. A woman on our team felt led to pray for this man. Following the method of prayer that we default to, unless led more specifically by the Holy Spirit, she interviewed him to find out what was wrong with his eyes. His eyes were white from about an eighth of an inch thickness of scar tissue that covered the entire pupil and cornea. Instead of Hispanic brown eyes, his were milky white. He was totally blind, having not seen a thing for fifty years.

The team member learned in the interview that as a five-year-old boy the man had accidently spilled muriatic acid in his eyes. Thus, his blindness was by a natural cause, so she ruled out psychosomatic blindness or an afflicting spirit. Then she spoke to the condition, commanding his eyes to be healed, for the scar tissue to disintegrate, and for the pupils and corneas to be reconstructed. After these prayers of command, she instructed the man to open his eyes to check if he could see anything.

When he opened his eyes, he could not see anything. She had initially felt led to go to this man and begin praying for him at the beginning of the service. She prayed for him throughout the hour of worship, the two hours of teaching and ministry by word of knowledge, and then for more than another hour during the time the team prays with the laying on of hands. She prayed for more than four hours for this one person.

There are usually so many people to pray for that I ask the team not to pray too long for any one person. (There were about six thousand people in the building that night.) Sometimes we are so overwhelmed with people wanting prayer that I instruct team members to pray for two people at a time, using both hands. We do not stay long with a single person unless something is clearly happening to him or her during the prayer time. Nothing was happening to this man.

Why did the woman stay and pray so long? She told someone on the team that every time she planned to stop and to pray for someone else, she heard a strong impression—"Do not stop praying." But when the night ended with so many blind and sick people healed, she left the man still totally blind. I wonder how she felt that night. I wonder if she questioned whether or not she had heard God correctly or if she had missed God's directives.

The next morning she left with the team to return to America and to the other countries represented by our Global team.

Three days later I flew from southern to northern Brazil to join another Global team. Soon after I arrived, my phone rang. The pastor from the church we had just left was on the phone. He was very excited. He told me the story I have just told you. Then he added, "This man could not see anything when the night was over. Neither could he see anything the next day and night, but on the third morning, though he went to bed totally blind, he woke up with brand-new eyes and clear vision."

Since the man's records were at the local hospital, everyone knew he had been blind for fifty years. The pastor told me, "He is right now down at the hospital for the third time. The doctors keep asking him, 'Tell us again, how is it you can see?'" (like the question asked in John 9 of the man born blind). He added, "This is the greatest miracle in the history of our city!"

These people—and many more—have become firm believers in God's promises of healing, And I'm sure that today, each one would enthusiastically testify, "LORD my God, I called to you for help, and you healed me" (Ps. 30:2). Will you call on Him today?

CHAPTER 2

THE LAME WALK

When John sent his disciples to ask Jesus for evidence that He was the foretold Messiah, Jesus told them, "Go back and report to John what you have seen and heard: . . . the lame walk" (Luke 7:18–22). I have personally witnessed "the lame walk" because of the power of God, still present and active today. This chapter tells their stories.

SCHEDULED FOOT AMPUTATION CANCELED

While I was ministering in Guarulhos, Brazil, one evening in 2011, I had a very faint and very brief impression. I wasn't sure, but I felt as if I heard the word *bicycle* or *motorcycle*. I had a follow-up impression that someone was present in the meeting who had been injured. I admit that the impression was so faint I wasn't sure it was from God, but I wanted to find out if I was right, so I gave the word of knowledge. I said, "I think there might be someone here who was injured either on a bicycle or a motorcycle."

Immediately I noticed a young woman who began to shake. She was located right in front of me, in about the third row, seated on the end chair. I knew she was the one. I left the platform and walked down to find out what was happening. I knew by her trembling that God was touching her. When I reached her seat, I noticed the calipers (crutches that wrap around the arms just above the elbows) that were lying on the floor under her chair. I also noticed she had a bandage that wrapped around one ankle and covered the Achilles' tendon and the heel.

I interviewed her and found out she had been in an accident while riding a motorcycle fifteen years earlier. Her heel had been caught in the spokes of the back wheel. This resulted in a large piece of flesh and muscle being ripped out of her heel and Achilles' tendon area. She had had several surgeries. Her doctor had attempted a muscle graft, which had failed. The lady now had a hole in her heel large enough and deep enough that you could put a golf ball in it. When she tried to walk without crutches, the injured area would tear even deeper into her foot. She had not been able to walk without crutches for fifteen years.

She had come to this church because she heard there was going to be a healing meeting. She didn't belong to the church; she was a Baptist, and this was a charismatic church of about eight thousand people. She had taken public transportation across the city of Saõ Paulo, which has about 45 million people. The reason she made this arduous trek was because the doctor had told her she needed to have her foot cut off in the coming week because it was becoming necrotic. The flesh was dying, and infection was setting in that would threaten her life if her foot wasn't amputated.

She had never heard of me, and I had not noticed her before giving this word of knowledge. I had not seen her come into the meeting on crutches. However, I knew it was the will of God to heal her because God had given me this word of knowledge, and by taking a risk and speaking it out, I found out I had been correct that someone had been hurt on a motorcycle. Also, the fact that the power of God was coursing through her body, causing her to slightly tremble, was encouraging to my faith. She not only told me her story but showed me pictures of the hole in her heel, which were quite graphic. (Later, when I showed the pictures in another church while telling her testimony, a young woman passed out and had to be carried out of the meeting.)

I began to pray for her. She told me she felt something happening in her heel. Then she told us that she felt as if she was supposed to try to walk without her crutches. When she attempted to do so, a smile spread across her face, because for the first time since the accident, she could walk without pain. She told us it felt like she was walking on marshmallows. The next day she was back at the church, dancing on the stage.

During the next few weeks, the entire hole began to fill in. The necrotic tissue turned from dark black dead tissue to pink. She did not need to have her foot amputated. A few years later she came to one of my meetings and danced onstage. She has since married.

I am so excited that I risked looking foolish and took the chance that I had heard from God at this church. By being willing to take that chance and step out in faith, I discovered I was correct. The word of knowledge created faith in this twenty-eight-year-old woman to be healed and created faith in me as a minister of healing as well. Even more exciting was that she was not the only person facing an amputation in less than a week who was healed. Two more women had likewise been told they needed amputations. Instead, they were healed and didn't have to undergo amputations of parts of their legs.[1]

SCHEDULED LEG AMPUTATION CANCELED

In 2010 I was in Uberlândia, Brazil, at a large church of several thousand. During the ministry time a woman asked for prayer. When I interviewed her to find out what her need was, she showed me her leg. Below the knee on the inside of her left leg was a large sore that had been infected for many years. She told us it was about four inches long and about one and a half inches wide. It was deep enough that you could see the bone. Doctors had tried many different types of antibiotics to kill the flesh-eating infection. Four doctors had concurred that the flesh was becoming necrotic and she needed to have her leg cut off just below her knee the following week.

When I began to pray for her, she told me she felt power going into her leg, especially in the area where the open sore was. I continued to pray several prayers for her healing, commanding the infection to die and the flesh to be restored.

One year later, when we returned to this church, the woman was there with a great smile of appreciation. She still had both legs. The bandage was gone, and you could see the area where the hole had formed in her leg. The flesh had grown back. She told me that when she went back to the doctors the week following the time of prayer, they were shocked to see the necrotic flesh had turned back to healthy flesh, and more important, the infection that the doctors had been unable to cure was dead. The doctors asked her what had happened. She told them she had been healed through prayer. Following is more of her story. (This is the translator's retelling of what Josilla had shared in Portuguese.)

Josilla came last year for prayer. She'd had a severe condition in her leg for about ten years. It was like an open ulcer. You could see the bone, because it was so deep. She was getting thrombosis. The bandages needed to be changed every other day, which cost her about eighty dollars each time, because it had to be performed by a doctor, who would take the bandages off, and then scrape the wound. It was terrible. The doctors had already decided to amputate the leg before the condition was able to spread further. When she came to the service a year ago, someone started to pray for her, and it felt like hot water was running down her leg.

Someone had a word of knowledge for her condition, so she took the bandages off. Randy prayed for her for about ten minutes, and the pain left. The swelling went down, and she has never put the bandages back on. After her healing, she was examined by a team of six doctors. Then they did another test. They removed some of the tissue to test it, and they found no infection. There is no pain, and [her scar] continues to get better and better.

QUADRIPLEGIC WOMAN HEALED FROM ADVANCED MULTIPLE SCLEROSIS

A few years later, I was in Brazil with another one of our ministry teams. (I always take a team with me when I go to Brazil. About half of the healings occur when the team ministers and half occur when I minister from the platform.) A computer programmer from New England, named Dennis McCormick, was on the team. During the ministry time, a woman's family had brought her to him. She was quadriplegic from advanced MS.

Dennis prayed for her for almost two hours, during which time she was gradually receiving healing. Though the healing was not instant, by the time Dennis finished praying, she was able to move her arms and legs, and could walk by herself. Dennis was addicted to the joy and excitement of seeing people healed when he prayed. During the next few years, he made several trips with me to Brazil. Later he moved to our headquarters in Mechanicsburg, Pennsylvania, and became one of my personal interns.

Many of the people on my team have experienced the outpouring of the Holy Spirit, enabling them to pray in the authority of Jesus' name and see healing and miracles in our day. Jesus did promise that we would do even greater works than He—if we will only believe (John 14:12). The power to lay hands on the sick and witness their recovery is just one of the many benefits of Jesus' crucifixion, resurrection, and ascension, and that power is available today—but only for "those who have believed" (Mark 16:15–18).

MIDDLE EASTERN QUADRIPLEGIC
MAN STANDS TO HIS FEET

My friend Leif Hetland, an apostolic evangelist who has a powerful healing gift and sees many miracles, shared the following two quadriplegic healing stories. The first one is of a man from a Middle Eastern country.

I received an assignment that was about to become mission impossible. That was to take the gospel of the kingdom to an area where there was no Christian witness. With a small team from America, we decided to do a healing explosion, and with fifty thousand posters, we invited any sick or oppressed people to come to a huge stadium and announced that Jesus was going to be there.

There was already a lot of tension and security concerns because of fear created in the atmosphere by previous suicide bombers. On the third night of our trip, with more than twenty-two thousand people in attendance with every type of disease possible, they were cramping and storming the stage. Every case of cancer, paralysis, blind eyes, deaf ears, and other conditions was present. Desperation was among the masses.

I still remember as the presence of Jesus started to spread across that huge field and explosions of joy rang out as people began to experience this presence. Through the presence of Jesus, creative miracles started to take place. Tumors were disappearing, blind eyes were opening, deaf ears were hearing, and the first two quadriplegics stood up—one from a wheelchair and one from a stretcher. This is visible on video footage taken at the event—it happened right in front of the stage.

The line of creative miracles alone was so long that we were unable to count the number, let alone count the other healings that were taking place. Jesus was showing us how good the Father is, and the presence of God was like a blanket of peace over the multitudes.

From a long distance as I stood on the stage, I saw a father lifting a wheelchair into the air. Then I saw him lower the wheelchair and then lift a young boy into the air. He then lowered the boy and raised the wheelchair again. It was an impossibility for him to get closer because of the crowd. My heart was broken as the security team grabbed hold of us and pushed us through the masses. Before we were crushed to death, they had to evacuate us from the venue to the vehicles.

I was still in shock at what had occurred, and after twenty-four hours, I ended up sitting in the Marriott, emotionally drained. I was grateful for what the Father had done, and yet at the same time, I was experiencing this deep pain for some of the people who had come to the meeting yet were unable to experience the breakthrough they longed for. One of the pictures that was engrained in my mind was that of the father with his young boy and the wheelchair.

Later that day, my coordinator in the Middle East received a phone call from the person who had organized the event. He said that a strange thing was happening. It had been twenty-four hours since we departed the event, but the presence continued to linger and affect people. So many stories had continued to take place. He gave an example of a father who had brought his son, a twelve-year-old quadriplegic. This Muslim father had heard the stories and testimonies and, with his last hope, he had brought his boy to the meeting hoping that this Jesus maybe could do something for his son.

The father had stood to the far left of the stage, holding up his son's wheelchair, and later on, his boy, hoping that someone would notice their need. That night, in deep disappointment, he'd rolled the boy home and laid his son on a mat on the floor.

Without the father's knowledge, throughout the night the presence of God was moving over this twelve-year-old boy and a creative miracle was taking place.

By early morning, the boy sensed movement in his hands and legs, and eventually, as the creative miracle took place, he had strength enough to do something he had never done before. He arose from his mat, walked into the kitchen, and hugged his father, totally healed. I cannot even think about this story without weeping. The faithfulness and the presence of Jesus still continues to work, and through that sweet kiss from Papa God, that little desire in my heart was being fulfilled.

QUADRIPLEGIC WOMAN IN IOWA WALKS AGAIN

In 2009 I was ministering in a church on a Sunday night in the Midwest. The service was over, and we were praying for many sick people. Close to 10:00 p.m., two people in wheelchairs came rolling down to the front. One of them had become paralyzed from the chest down as a result of a car accident seven years earlier. I was tired, and also the person in the chair was tired. I was thinking about how I could get to the hotel room as fast as possible, when the pastor turned to me and said, "There are a few more people to pray for before you leave." I walked up to the young lady in the wheelchair—let's call her Janet—and introduced myself.

Following a car accident at the age of eighteen, she had been prayed for by different people: Bill Johnson, Randy Clark, and myself, to name a few. The fact that she was still in a wheelchair didn't help my faith level.

I asked Janet, "What would you like the Father to do for you?"

She replied, "I want him to heal my orphan spirit."

My heart as a father of three daughters was suddenly bleeding. I realized that when someone has been prayed for hundreds of times with no breakthrough, she feels more like an orphan than a beloved daughter.

I asked Janet if it would be okay if I released a baptism of love so that she would know how much Papa God loves her and that it is His pleasure to heal her. Janet nodded in agreement. After releasing the prayer, I asked the Holy Spirit for a sign that Janet was going to be healed. The honest truth was that I looked at her body and asked what was going to be easiest. I asked her, "Would you be able to move your finger?" She said no. I told her that we were going to ask the Father, as a beloved daughter of the One who wants to heal her, for a sign that He was going to heal her tonight.

I asked her if we could believe together that she would be able to move one inch with her left hand. She agreed. I prayed and nothing happened. I prayed a second time, a third time, and by the fourth time, she still hadn't felt anything. But then I could see her fingers starting to move, and a spark came into her eyes. I said, "Do you believe that God is tired?" to which she replied, "No," and so we continued to pray.

First we prayed for her left hand to open, then the other hand. Then we prayed for her to be able to lift them above her head. Each time we saw that specific breakthrough. We continued this process, and step-by-step, we continued to pray and asked for more. I asked the senior pastor to come and join us, and by this time there were about twenty-five to thirty people watching.

It took about one hour and forty-five minutes before Janet stood up from the chair and took the first step. It took less than twenty minutes from the first step before she was running around the sanctuary, with the children chasing her. Her father and sister came. [Her father] was an evangelical who didn't believe that God still performed miracles. He was astonished by the goodness and kindness of God.

By the following service word had spread about what God had been doing, and it was filled up as Janet walked all the way to the front of the stage and shared her testimony. The place exploded in radical worship. That was my first time seeing a major creative miracle in America and the beginning of me believing that the Jesus I have seen in Africa, the Middle East, and Asia is the same Jesus in America.

POLICE OFFICER WITH SEVERED SPINE JUMPS OUT OF WHEELCHAIR

In August 2003 we were in Manaus, a city of about a million, deep within the Amazon rain forest in northern Brazil. It was our first night to minister. On the bus en route to the church with my ministry team of eighty members, I asked them, "How many of you have had words of knowledge for healing?" Nearly three-fourths of the team had never had a word of knowledge. I then asked them, "How many of you have prayed for someone's healing and seen them healed?" Again, three-fourths of the team had never seen a healing when they prayed. I told them, "I believe before forty-eight hours is over, every one of you will have a word of knowledge for healing and will have prayed for someone who is healed."

It happened—within forty-eight hours, every one of them had received a word of knowledge and saw someone healed when they prayed.

That evening, around eleven o'clock, the ministry team and I having given words of knowledge and seen hundreds healed through prayer from the platform, I had the ministry team go down on the floor. They formed a long line across the front of the sanctuary, which seated one thousand people. I then invited the people to come to the front and to tell our team what they needed healed. My team would lay hands on them and pray for their healing. (There were some translators, and our team had learned a few Portuguese phrases useful in praying for the sick.)

As the people were coming forward, one of the team members— we'll call him Sam—became very nervous. He had never prayed for anyone in his life. In fact, he had joined the team to gain the experience of praying for the sick. His wife had been with us on other trips, and she had returned home telling him of all the healings she witnessed.

A recovering alcoholic, he had wanted to come for three years, but each year, shortly before the trip, he would fall off the wagon. Ashamed, he would not go on the trip. This year he had maintained his sobriety.

As the people were coming forward, he prayed this prayer: "God, You know I have never prayed for anyone, I don't know what I am doing, so please bring me an easy one—a headache or a bellyache."

Sam looked out into the crowd and saw a young man in a wheel-chair coming toward him. He prayed, "No, Lord, not that! An easy one, a headache or a bellyache." He looked away, not wanting to make eye contact with the young man. But moments later, the young man tugged on his trousers.

Though Sam had never prayed for anyone, all the team members had been given instruction through videos and books on how to pray for the sick. He interviewed the paraplegic and found out he was a twenty-five-year-old police officer. He had been shot in the stomach, and the bullet had severed his spinal cord.

Sam's flight had been canceled in Atlanta, and he had been up all night in the airport and then flew to Saõ Paulo and on to Manaus. He had not slept in almost forty-eight hours. As he was praying for the paraplegic, he was growing sleepy. He interviewed him again to see if anything was happening in response to his prayer. The paraplegic told him, "No, nothing is happening." Sam, who had only a little faith to start with, now realized he had no faith.

Then he remembered a statement I had written in the *Ministry Team Training Manual*: "I don't expect you to heal anyone, only God can heal, but I do expect you to love the people, and to treat them with respect." He thought to himself, *I haven't prayed very long for this young man; if I stop now, he will feel like he isn't valued. Even though I don't have faith for him to be healed, I can take the time to pray for him so he will feel valued and loved.*

As the night was getting later, Sam was becoming sleepier. He said, "My head was now resting on the paraplegic's shoulder, and just before I started to snore, the young man jumped out of the wheelchair, grabbed me, put his face on my shoulder, and wet my shirt with his tears. Then he walked off, pushing the wheelchair." We didn't catch this happening. It is difficult to catch a healing on camera when it happens when you have a team of eighty people. But the next day we videoed the young man's testimony.[2]

PARAPLEGIC MAN FROM CAR ACCIDENT

On another international ministry trip, I was in Belém, Brazil, a city in the north near the Amazon and on the Atlantic Ocean. This is the city where the first Pentecostal missionaries came from the

United States, in 1909, and the beginning of the Assemblies of God denomination in Brazil, which is older than the Assemblies of God in the United States.[3] I was working with the Foursquare denomination, Quadrangular in Brazil. There were more than twenty-five thousand people in the open-air crusade. It was held in a corral-type arena without any seats. Everyone stood for the entire service, which lasted for three nights in a row. Even in the pouring rain one night, they still packed the arena.

Our plane had been delayed, and the meeting had already begun when we arrived. I did not know the lead pastor who had organized the meeting. During the first night some of the local church's ministry team had claimed people had been healed. They held up several wheelchairs, and then placed the wheelchairs on the stage. When the meeting was over, I was sickened to see those same people come and get their wheelchairs and sit in them to be taken from the meeting. They had not really been healed. I felt so embarrassed by this deception.

After the last night I was talking with the adult son of the lead pastor who was over the Quadrangular denomination for the state, with hundreds of churches. He asked me what I thought of the meetings. There had been hundreds of healings. He was very excited, and they were inviting me back to do another crusade. I told him that it was good, but I was disappointed. I had wanted to see some miracles, blind eyes opened, deaf ears hearing, especially someone walking out of a wheelchair.

I was assured that there had been a man healed of paralysis who had been paraplegic for five years. The pastor's son asked, "Didn't you see the wheelchair being lifted in the air?" Then I told him what I had seen the first night, and how sickened I was when I realized the declaration of people healed had not really happened. I said, "Yes, I saw the wheelchair lifted in the air, but I was afraid it wasn't really true, that it was another incident of claiming a healing that really hadn't happened. That is why I didn't draw any attention to the wheelchair raised overhead by leaders of your church."

He responded, "Randy, I personally know that man. He has not been able to move below his waist due to a car accident five years ago. That was a genuine healing. He is walking."

I agreed to come back and hold another crusade. I was so excited that a paraplegic had been healed.

BRAZILIAN WOMAN'S LEG HEALED

Also in 2010 in Brazil, a woman named Milena reported having a motorcycle accident eight years earlier, which broke her tibia. As a result, one leg was three inches shorter than the other one. It then became infected. The infection was so bad, doctors were going to amputate the leg. They removed a tendon from her right knee and replaced a tendon on her left knee. Surgeons had to put large screws in her knee to keep the tendons in place.

In the summer of 2009, Milena received prayer from the Youth Power Invasion team. She then went to the doctor, but the doctor found that the screw was gone. Now, her shortened leg caused her back pain, but during prayer the leg grew out. Today, she no longer limps or has pain.

• • •

The grace of God, revealed in healing, has been exhibited in these stories. I pray that your faith to experience this goodness of God's grace for yourself has been strengthened. Jesus is "the same yesterday and today and forever" (Heb. 13:8). May you believe Him for—and receive—your own healing today.

CHAPTER 3

THE SICK ARE HEALED

M any an afflicted person has taken comfort and gained hope from Psalm 107:20, which says, "He [God] sent out his word and healed them." In this chapter I will share the stories of several who once were sick but now are whole, precisely because He sent His word and healed them. God continues to send His specific words to believers today as confirmation that the healing they have prayed for has been granted, or as words of knowledge indicating what God specifically has chosen to heal in a particular setting. This word from the Lord reveals His will, causing either a greater measure of faith or the gift of faith to come to the one in need of healing. In this way the word of the Lord causes faith to increase, resulting in the gift of healing.

WOMAN HEALED OF SEPTIC SHOCK AND INFECTION

On June 9, 2004, Susan Starr's body experienced trauma when scar tissue from a surgery seven years earlier choked off her colon; it turned gangrenous and burst inside of her while she was outside in the garden.

Susan had a lot of health issues before this incident, so she had a high pain tolerance. In fact, at the time her colon was becoming infected, she was teaching second grade, having a fine time. When it burst, she went into septic shock. Her arms and legs curled up, which occurred, she learned later, to preserve her head and heart. She stayed that way until the paramedics gave her oxygen.

Susan's nervous system really suffered. That night she underwent surgery to remove two to three feet of colon. Doctors weren't sure she would survive.

After the surgery, when her body was healing, she kept fainting. The doctors told her that her nervous system was "fried." She had to take a pill in the morning to keep her heartbeat from becoming too rapid, and she had to take one at night to keep it from beating too slowly. She had to take many pills, some for blood pressure, others for temperature, breathing, digestion, and blood flow. She suffered from at least ten to fifteen bouts of diarrhea each day, spending around two hours in the bathroom. She was taking forty-five to fifty-five pills a day, including pain medication.

Susan says the pain was so excruciating because her blood circulation never went all the way to her feet. When she woke up in the morning, her arms and legs were blue and purple. She had to stop teaching because she continually fainted and had to lie down for the rest of the day. She was on a strict diet, and her activities were very limited. Doctors told her that her disease was progressive and terminal. As years went on, different organs were affected, and they showed deterioration. She had a few more surgeries and organs removed.

All during that time she was looking for a healing. She was even teaching a Bible study—on healing. She wanted to be healed of all her afflictions. She wrote Psalm 118:17, "I will not die but live," on a piece of paper and carried it with her wherever she went.

One of Susan's surgeries required her to remain in the hospital overnight. She had a notepad by her bed, and by the next morning she noticed she had written "Randy Clark" five times. She didn't know who that was, so she started asking everyone she knew. One of her friends told her who I was. Susan called me and tried to get an appointment, but I was traveling. Susan looked at my itinerary and saw I was soon to come to High Point, North Carolina, for a Healing School, which was near her home.

After her discharge, Susan was not doing well. She had a wheelchair and a walker she used when she left her house. The doctor told her husband around that time to prepare for death and say good-bye. Susan had started to clear out her things and give them away. In April 2013, Susan was put in hospice care, per her doctor's suggestion.

But when the Healing School came to her town, Susan made it to the conference, and she went to the front. But she couldn't make it the whole time, and she left after an hour and a half. She slept the rest of the day and through the night.

The next morning she got up, got dressed, and went back to High Point. After about five or ten minutes at the conference, her friend came over to her and said that Rodney Hogue would pray for her. She sat with Rodney and told him she wanted him to say, "You are healed in the name of Jesus!" When Susan told him all that was wrong, he began to pray for her. He called out all her body parts from the top of her head to her feet. Susan says that as he prayed for her, she felt something like "gold hot chocolate" running through her.

When Rodney spoke to her lungs, she felt "liquid gold" and knew something was happening. When he called out her colon, she could feel it moving. She had no control over her feet, and she just felt very warm. She felt as if she were floating, and she realized she had no pain. Her friends laid her down on a mat at the front of the church. She remembers hearing, "Go to Brazil" while she lay on that mat.

She got up and went into the lunchroom. There she saw a buffet of all the foods she could not eat at the time. She thought it was a test from the Lord. She piled up her plate and sat down and ate it all. That's when she realized she had been healed, and she felt amazing.

That night she drove to the airport to pick up her husband. She hadn't told him anything that happened. As soon as he saw her, he jumped up and down with her, and he screamed, "Susan, you've been healed!"

Susan went back to the healing conference, and her friends ran up to me and told me that Susan was healed. I brought her up onstage. The week before she was bed bound. But standing next to me, she gave her testimony. At the next break, four people showed up to be prayed for by Susan. Susan prayed for them, and they began to fall over. She went to the bathroom, and there a woman asked for prayer. Susan prayed for her, and the woman slumped down to the floor.[1]

Ever since the day she was healed, she has noticed that whenever God wants to heal someone, her hands feel as if they are on fire.[2]

TRINITY MUSIC CITY, TENNESSEE— ADVANCED PARKINSON'S HEALED

The first time I saw someone healed of Parkinson's disease was in 1994 or 1995. I was at Trinity Music City, in Hendersonville, Tennessee. This was the hardest series of meetings I had for the entire year. I was on the twenty-third day of a forty-day fast. I was fasting with the specific focus of getting a breakthrough in seeing creative miracles. On this night I was preaching on impartation, especially for those who were twenty-nine and younger. The invitation was for those who felt called to become pastors, church planters, missionaries, worship leaders, or evangelists to come to the altar. I was going to lay hands on them and bless what the Holy Spirit was doing in their lives. I told the congregation, "Tonight, only tonight, I am not going to pray for the sick. If you need prayer for healing, go up to the balcony, where my team will pray for you. I am only praying for these young people who are dedicating their lives to ministry tonight."

Shortly after this announcement, while I was praying for the young people, a woman named Anne came up to me asking me to pray for her. Her husband, Elvis, stood behind her. Anne was only forty-nine but looked like she was sixty. She was trembling. (At that time there were many people in our meetings who were shaking, but shaking due to the anointing of the Holy Spirit.)

I told her, "I'm not praying for healings tonight, only for impartation. Didn't you hear what I just said?" She replied, "Yes, and I went to the balcony for prayer. I wasn't healed, and I believe God told me that if you would pray for me, He would heal me." (At the time I didn't believe it was really God, but only her imagination, so I didn't want to pray for her. But I have found it sometimes is easier to pray a short prayer and then go on with what you feel that God is telling you to do.)

I asked her, "What is wrong? What is your problem?" She replied, "I have Parkinson's disease. I shake so hard I have never held my two-year-old grandson. I don't have a short-term memory. I can't remember a telephone number. I can't walk without leaning on my husband, and I am losing control of my bladder. The other day I was in the grocery store and peed all over myself. I am taking $280 a month for medication. I need to be in a nursing home, and we can't afford it. I won't live like this. I need to be healed."

I reached my hand toward her forehead and said, "Come, Holy Spirit." Before I could say anything more, she had fallen to the floor. She was lying there, not shaking. I asked Elvis if that was normal. He replied, "No, the only time she doesn't shake is when she is in a deep sleep." I thought, *Well, maybe being slain in the Holy Spirit is like a deep sleep.*

I walked away to continue ministering to the young people who had come forward for prayer. But I was intrigued with what was happening to this woman. So I walked back to Elvis and asked him, "Elvis, what is Parkinson's?" He replied, "It is a disease that kills brain cells, and she has 800 million cells that have been destroyed."

When Elvis said this, I became very excited. I realized I was on the twenty-third day of a fast to see creative miracles. I came off the stage and knelt beside her. I lifted up my left hand as I placed my right hand on her forehead. I prayed, "O God, I call those things that are not as though they were. In the name of Jesus, I ask You for 800 million new brain cells!"

When I said this, Anne, who had been lying quietly on the floor, began to writhe, yelling, "Stop praying! Stop praying! My head—it's killing me!" I prayed, "Oh, God, don't listen to her prayer; listen to mine. More! More! More!"

Then she went perfectly still. I leaned over and whispered in her ear. "What is happening?" She responded, "I don't feel anything. I don't hear anything"—and there was a lot of noise going on, with much prayer happening all around us. "All I know is that you are here, Jesus is here, and Elvis is here."

Then she began to lift up her right hand, extending her arm its full length. She was turning her hand over from front to back, staring at her hand. She was watching it not shake! Then she began to take her left arm and move it in a half circle, ending with her pointer finger on the tip of her nose. She did this many times. Elvis looked at me and said, "Do you know what she is doing?" I said, "No, what is she doing?" Elvis responded, "That is a test for Parkinson's; she hasn't been able to do that for several years."

She then raised herself up on one elbow and asked Elvis to get her a cup of water. When he returned, she drank it. They were both excited. I thought, *Big deal. She drank water.* Then Elvis, realizing I did not appreciate the moment, looked at me and said, "She had lost the ability to drink from a cup; she could only sip through a straw."

She asked, "Can I go up on the stage?" I thought, *God just healed her. She is queen for a day; she can do anything she wants.*

Once up on the stage, she turned and grabbed Elvis's hand,

squeezed it, and said, "I'm squeezing my husband's hand!" She stomped her foot three times upon the stage, then took a step toward the edge of the stage. Looking into the eyes of the congregation, she said, "I haven't held my grandson, who is two years old. They were afraid I would drop him with all my shaking. I'm going to go home and hold him. I have been spending $280 a month on medicine. Just think what Elvis and I are going to do with all that money."

Then she turned toward me and said, "Do you have a piano?" I said, "No, but we have a keyboard." "Can I play it?" she asked. I told her, "Of course." I didn't know if she could play or not, but we walked over to the keyboard, and she began to play it. She actually played the piano quite well.

Elvis came up beside me with tears in his eyes. He said to me, "Seven years ago I was singing, and my wife would accompany me on the piano. In the middle of a song, she stopped, not able to think of a note or a chord. Embarrassed, she ran out of the building through a side door. The next week we went to the doctor's office and they diagnosed her with Parkinson's disease."

This was the first time in seven years her hands had touched a keyboard.

Then, she began to sing. This was her husband's gift, not hers! But no one cared. We had seen a creative miracle take place in front of our eyes. Anne's brain had been regenerated. No one cared that she sang off-key. Everyone began to join her as she sang.

There wasn't a dry eye in the house.

HEALED OF PANCREATIC CANCER— WITH JUST WEEKS TO LIVE

In 1995 I was at Evangel, the largest Assemblies of God church in Kentucky, pastored by Bob Rodgers. I was preaching a renewal meeting.

During the ministry time a mechanic from Georgia brought to me a young man named Tony Ellis. He asked if I would pray for Tony. When I looked at Tony, I knew he had some form of cancer.

I asked him, "What is wrong with you? What do you need to be healed of?" He told me, "I have pancreatic cancer. I am twenty-three and am a male nurse. I have done all that could be done medically for the treatment, and I only have a few weeks to live." He also told me that he was a nominal Roman Catholic.

I told him that I was going to pray for him. I said, "Tony, I don't want you to pray while I am praying for you. I want you to relax and focus on your body. If you begin to feel anything, let me know. About 50 percent of the people who are healed feel something, but the other 50 percent who are healed do not feel anything. My faith is not in your feelings, but in God. However, if you do feel something, tell me, for it will encourage me and help me know how to better pray for you."

When I began to pray for him, it was not long before I saw the power of God come upon him. He began to tremble under the power of God. When this happened, I was greatly encouraged because I knew that the Lord had showed up, and His power was touching Tony. I just rested in a peaceful delight, knowing God was touching him. Occasionally I would say, "God, I bless what You are doing. I bless Your power that is touching Tony."

After about fifteen minutes the trembling and the heat stopped. Tony stood up to leave, thanking me for the prayer. I said, "Tony, I don't think you should leave yet. I think there may be more that God wants you to do. Why don't we just wait for five minutes, allowing time for God to touch you again."

Tony agreed. He sat back down, and I once again prayed, "Lord, we don't want to miss what You are doing. If there is more You want to do in Tony's life, then we position ourselves to receive it. Father, if there is more, show Tony or me." Shortly after praying this, the Spirit fell upon Tony again.

Tony experienced several cycles of being touched by God's electrical power for fifteen to twenty minutes, followed by feeling nothing for about five minutes before another round would start. I prayed for Tony three to four times a day. Each time he experienced several of these cycles.

Then, on the last day, the last time I prayed for Tony, he saw what looked like a fireball coming toward him. It hit him and went into his body. This completed the healing.

Several weeks later I was visiting the church and happened to be there to see Tony being baptized. He had been totally healed.

Tony became an evangelist and sometimes prayed for the sick during his meetings.

BRAZILIAN WOMAN CURED
OF STAGE 4 CANCER

My vice president, Tom Jones, prayed for a woman in Ribeirão, Preto, Brazil, who was in the last stages of cancer. Her body was not responding to traditional medical treatment. But when she was prayed for, she was instantly healed.

When she went back to the doctor, he couldn't believe it. He asked her what had happened. What had she done? She said, "God has healed me!" The doctor told her he wanted to study her case, to try to find out how God had healed her.

A few months later, I was in the same church and she came forward to give her testimony of healing. She said that her doctor was so excited because nothing more could have been done, medically speaking, for her condition. He told her, "I know God has healed you."

GOD USES TWELVE-YEAR-OLD BOY
TO HEAL VETERAN OF CANCER

Bill Johnson tells the story of a Sacramento Valley veteran who had received a report that he was dying of cancer. His son, who was a believer, encouraged him to come to Bethel Church in Redding, California, to receive prayer, but he was an unbeliever, so he said no.

In time, the cancer got worse and worse, so he finally gave in, just to go. He came into the room, but he was not happy to be there. He was not open or hungry or full of faith. He was there to satisfy his son.

The prayer group came to pray for him, and he said, "You can pray for me, but don't touch me." He just rested for a moment while they prayed for him, and he closed his eyes.

Then, a twelve-year-old walked over and touched his chest, and he fell back to the floor. Angry, he said, "Who pushed me?" But when he saw it was a kid, he said, "Okay" and got up. It's unclear how much he realized in the moment, but he did understand that no one had pushed him. The power of God had hit him. When he went back to the doctor, he learned that he didn't have cancer anymore. But even more exciting to me is what happened afterward.

He went back to the doctor again and told him and some of his assistants that he went to Bethel. He had printed out a brochure with his testimony and with a map to Bethel on the back, and he handed it out.

From then on, he would bring carloads of people every week to receive prayer. He had to carry one lady to the front because she was in such pain. She got completely healed. He had driven her to the service, but on the way home, she told him to pull over, and she drove the rest of the way. He brought several people to the services, and to my knowledge, all of them got healed.

This veteran gave his life to the Lord, and he moved to Redding and is part of our ministry team now. Before, he was a tough biker guy who was very resistant to anything to do with God, but now he is a tender, joyful man.

REX BURGHER OF MONTANA
HEALED OF SCLEROSIS

The following testimony was written by a man who could surely echo the words of Joseph: "You intended to harm me, but God intended it for good" (Gen. 50:20). God doesn't make people sick. It is the thief, the devil, who comes "to steal and kill and destroy" (John 10:10). But God can surely turn what Satan intended for harm into something "good," to the glory of God. That's what happened for Rex. Once smitten with disease, today he prays for healing for those with the very disease that once held him captive. Here's his story, in his own words.

When an unexpected illness comes upon you, you are often faced with questions as to "Why?" Whether the condition stems from either a physical, emotional, or spiritual condition or a combination thereof, often the body reacts and a physical illness ensues. Sometimes it is hard to know what caused the illness, but over time a person's perspective begins to sort out the events that happened around the time the illness occurred that gives insight into the possible root cause of the illness. Often to see God working you have to look back and see what He's done.

For me it first began in 1994, a year before God poured out His Spirit on our family and began to use us to spread revival in the CMA Church and throughout Montana. It started innocently enough when a stranger happened to ask me where I went to church. I told him and he said, "Oh! You are Baha'i Faith!"

"Why would you say that?" I asked.

"Because you have the Baha'i Faith symbols over your build-ing," he answered.

"What symbols?" I said.

"Those two interlocking circles over the building, those represent the Baha'i Faith religion," he said.

I was an elder and had attended the church for close to four years and knew nothing about the meaning of the symbols that were perched at the top of our church. I just thought they were part of the design over the entryway. Having found out what they really stood for and that they had been allowed to remain was beyond my comprehension. Two nights later at an elders' meeting, I asked the pastors and other elders if they knew about this. "Oh yes!" they all said. "The architect of the building was Baha'i Faith, and he put those symbols on top of the building. We were hoping to reach him for Christ, so we just let him do it." I couldn't believe what I was hearing but was even more exasperated when they told me he had not become a Christian and still they had left the symbols up there.

"I'm going to take those symbols down because people think we are a Baha'i Faith church," I said. However, in classic church leadership fashion, they said they didn't oppose the idea but would have to pass it on to the governing board to see if there was any money available to do the job.

I looked at them and said, "I have the money and I'll have a crane here this week to take those symbols down." By the end of the week, the symbols were on their way to the dump.

Interestingly enough, it was not long after that I began to feel a pain in the little toe of my left foot. It was a strange sensation and felt like someone had grabbed hold of it, was pulling it out and twisting it at the same time. Within a few days, the pain traveled up my left leg to the calf, turning into a numbing sensation. Naturally everyone told me to go to a chiropractor, which I did. He worked me over pretty good and took a few diagnostic tests, but nothing changed. After he was done, he told me that he did everything he knew to do and that I should go see my family doctor.

It took two weeks to get in to see him, and by then the numbness had jumped to the other leg and all the way up to my waist. By the time we could see a doctor, I was numb from the waist down. It felt like someone had given me a huge shot of Novocain that affected the entire middle of my body.

After I finally made it in to see the doctor, he decided that I needed to see a neurologist, who immediately ordered an MRI. Now close to four weeks had gone by since I first noticed a twinge in my little toe.

The next day, after the MRI, the doctor had my wife and me come into his office and he showed us the MRIs and pointed to a sclerosis on my back. By this time the numbness was in my feet, making it difficult for me to walk. As we talked, I mentioned that I was in need of new glasses to see better, which alarmed the neurologist, who immediately ordered a brain MRI and a spinal tap. It was at the end of the day but they were able to get me in for an MRI that day. As we were getting ready to proceed down to get the MRI, he told me that he thought another sclerosis had formed and that I would probably lose my vision and live my remaining life in a darkened state. There is nothing like good news to bring cheer to a patient's day; to say our time that night at home was a somber affair would be an understatement.

The next morning we met the doctor, who had by now reviewed the test results. He proceeded to tell us what the next steps would be in fighting the sclerosis in my back that was causing the numbness. Finally, after ten minutes or so, I stopped him and asked him what the test results were from the brain MRI. He said, "Oh, those! They turned out fine; you have no sign of any more sclerosis in your brain." Frankly, I could have reached over and slapped him alongside his head. The words that he had used before the test had scared us and caused a lot of stress without really knowing for sure, and I considered that cruel and unusual punishment.

It turned out that there was only one sclerosis, so it was not multiple sclerosis, but the numbness continued to increase until I had zero feeling around my waist and my legs had become so numb that I was almost in need of a cane.

It was during the spinal tap that our pastor and one of the elders came in, anointed me with oil, and prayed for me. Lois (my wife) felt that something significant had happened while they prayed for me, and she was sure that God had answered their prayers. Lois then prayed to cancel any demonic spirits that would have any right to attack me. However, since we were not sure that I was healed, I continued to take the medicine the doctors prescribed and followed their instructions until we could see if God had really healed me. I myself did not feel anything significant had happened to me as they prayed over me. I knew Lois was sure that something did happen, and having prayed for many people through the years and seen them receive their healing even months later, I knew that if God had indeed touched me I would soon be experiencing some measure of healing—if not a complete restoration, then a stop to the downward spiral that I was experiencing.

Praise God, our prayers were answered; not only did the downward spiral stop, but something supernatural happened. With a sclerosis, the best you can hope for is that another sclerosis will not appear. A sclerosis does irrevocable damage to a section of nerve endings that run throughout your spine. It is like having a series of junction boxes that are filled with electrical wires positioned up and down your spine. When one of those boxes suddenly becomes fried, it affects a different part of your body. One electrical box is a sclerosis; when several are fried, it is called multiple sclerosis. Once it has been fried, there is just no chance that you can go in and repair the circuits that were damaged. So having the symptoms that are a result of the sclerosis disappear is not heard of, but that is what happened to me. The only thing that remains is an occasional twinge in my little toe on my left foot, which I first experienced perhaps as a reminder of God's grace on my life.

I was blessed to be healed; it was confirmation to us that the hand of God was on me. Looking back, we believe the physical attack on me and subsequently my family was in direct relationship to removing the occult symbols over the church. The enemy wanted to take me out before the coming outpouring of the Holy Spirit on our family. Because of this our life plans were altered, which positioned us for the events to take place that enabled us to be used powerfully of God around the world.

Before this all happened, our family had planned on an extended horseback trip to the Black Hills for the summer. With our one-ton crew cab truck, camper, and four-horse trailer and horses, we were good to go, but the sclerosis held us back. The last time I went to see my doctor, I asked him if he thought we could go on the horseback trip, and he gave me the go-ahead, but with the cautious statement, "Whatever you do, protect that back of yours."

That afternoon after returning home, I went out and saddled up a new horse that I had been riding previous to the first sclerosis. As I got settled in to the saddle, he reared up, and with his eyes rolled back in his head, he began to backpedal as fast as he could and flipped over in the air. I knew I was close to the hitching post and twisted my back just enough to have it hit my shoulder instead of directly on my back. I came to rest there, with the horse coming down on my leg. One last attempt to take me out was what I realized had happened. I never rode the horse again and put him up for sale, and we never took the horse vacation that we had planned. Instead we went to Canada for a family vacation, and it was then that the Holy Spirit led us to visit our worship leader, who, being Canadian, was awaiting the necessary paperwork to return to the States. When we decided to turn to go toward his home rather than continue our vacation, the Holy Spirit filled the cab of our truck, and during our time at his home, the Spirit became as intense to us as any other time in our lives. He was also the person who later gave us the brochure to go to a conference, "Let the River Flow" in Kelowna, British Columbia, that was instrumental in our being used of God.

When you take the time to look back over your life, you can see the hand of God leading you to a place of destiny and purpose. From the beginning of our story, God's hand has been upon us. If at any time we had allowed the enemy the opportunity to discourage us enough to give up, it's possible none of what we are writing about would have happened.

The good news is that God has used us powerfully in praying for others with MS, and not only were some healed, but many experienced a substantial restoration of their conditions caused by the sclerosis.

Praise God![3]

MAN HEALED OF PTSD

In a meeting in Redding, California, a man was healed of post-traumatic stress disorder (PTSD) in one of our meetings. I had been handing out books on identity, and this man felt that he should ask me personally what this book was about. I told him the title of the book, and he told me he had lost his identity in war. I felt at that point that if I walked away from him, he would leave. So, I took off my mic and sat with him. He didn't come to the meeting to be healed of PTSD, but rather for his nerve pain. He wanted the pain gone so he could live a normal life.

Mike Hutchings came to pray for him, and Mike wouldn't let him put his head down; he made him look in his eyes. The man had been carrying guilt and shame on him from what he had seen in his time in the service. He went to his doctor and asked if PTSD could be cured because at that time he was even considering taking his own life. But after prayer with Mike, walking through the stages of healing, in a short prayer, just five minutes, he felt peace and Jesus' presence. From that moment on, he was healed both physically and from the emotional effects of severe PTSD, from which the doctors had told him it would be impossible to recover.[4]

FIRST CASE OF SCHIZOPHRENIA HEALING

My church in the St. Louis area had started a small group support ministry for people who had medical diagnoses of a mental disease. The group was growing, as few churches provided such a ministry. I was becoming more and more aware of the suffering experienced by those with mental illness.

Not seeing a breakthrough in the area of healing for mental illness, while we were seeing a lot of physical illness being healed, I began to have my associate and assistant pastors join me as we walked through the sanctuary, praying over every chair and quoting and declaring Psalm 103:2–3: "Praise the LORD, my soul, and forget not all his benefits—who forgives all your sins and heals all your diseases." I would tell the Lord, "Your Word says '*all your diseases*,' not just 'your physical diseases.' Lord, we ask for a breakthrough in mental illness as well. I believe You can heal any kind of illness, any kind of mental illness." We saw the Lord begin to heal mental illnesses, but our Goliath that seemed to mock the army of God was schizophrenia.

I asked several friends who had healing ministries if they had ever seen schizophrenia healed. At that time none of them had; one of them even had a brother who had been stricken with schizophrenia. Another friend and pastor had a child who suffered from it.

In my travel to more than fifty nations, I had only heard, at that time, of two people who had been healed of schizophrenia: one instantly, in Argentina, in the ministry of Omar Cabrera, and the other during six months of prayer and counseling.

The first breakthrough in the healing of schizophrenia, in my ministry, occurred in Tuscon, Arizona. I was conducting a healing school for my friend Bob Sawvelle, pastor of Passion Church.

A young woman of about twenty-eight had suffered from schizo-phrenia for about seven years. She had graduated high school with the highest SAT scores in the state, then graduated on a scholastic scholarship from Virginia University, when she was stricken with the disease. It had reduced her to a shell of her former self. She could not function alone. Her parents had provided her a small apartment, but her mom would have to tell her to eat, to bathe, to do the simple things we all take for granted. She had lost the ability to speak in complete sentences. Her first name was Julie.

I was preaching a message titled "A Biblical Basis for Healing." I felt that God had told me He would heal people as I taught the Bible. And for almost twenty-two years, every time I gave this message, people would be healed during the message. The first time I taught the message, I got the impression that God was telling me to tell the people that if they felt the presence of God come on their bodies during the sermon, they should stand up until I saw them and said, "I bless you in the name of Jesus." Then they could sit back down. At the end of the message, I wanted those who had stood to check out their bodies, and for those who could verify they had been healed by their pain leaving or their lost function restored to wave their hands over their heads until their hands crossed.

So on this particular night, there was a staff pastor of a seven-thousand-member Southern Baptist church present who had enjoyed my teachings—up to now. However, he did not like this message; he was skeptical and thought it was somewhat showy. Yet, while he did not personally like the message, he had a strong impression. *Stand up!* This impression came several times. He resisted, thinking, *I don't feel anything—I don't need healing.* But then he heard another impression, and he realized it was not about his healing, but about the healing of his stepdaughter, Julie. He left the meeting to get her and bring her to the meeting. When he arrived, the ministry time was occurring, and Pastor Bob Sawvelle laid hands on Julie's forehead and simply said, "I bless you in Jesus' name." Julie undoubtedly felt something. But the greatest degree of healing came that night, when she was in her apartment.

Once at home, Julie thought she heard God speak to her in an impression. *Anoint your head with oil.* Julie found oil and anointed her head. Then she heard the impression, *Now anoint your whole body with oil.* Julie removed her clothes and anointed her whole body with oil. When she obeyed, the power of God came upon her and she fell to the floor under the power. She felt electricity go through her body the whole night as she lay on the floor under the power of God. When morning came, Julie was healed of schizophrenia.[5]

SECOND SCHIZOPHRENIC HEALED

The second healing of schizophrenia also happened to a young woman in her twenties. It was 2015 and occurred in Oshawa, Canada. I was conducting a mini-school for healing for my friend Pastor Doug

Schneider, an apostolic leader among the Pentecostal Assemblies of Canada. I had him follow up with the mother and her daughter. He spent almost an hour in the follow-up and could not see any signs of the schizophrenia in the young woman.

The mother came to me late in the evening after I had taught on healing and was praying for the sick. She said, "I have my daughter back." She was very emotional, with her eyes full of tears. I said, "What do you mean?" She responded, "My daughter had schizophrenia. She was a bright student in university when she was stricken with it. She had been in several psychiatric hospitals. I had to quit my good job and could only work part-time because I have had to spend so much time taking care of my daughter."

Then she told me that my book had brought about her daughter's healing. I had just released a new book, titled *The Biblical Guidebook to Deliverance* (Lake Mary, FL: Charisma House, 2015). This was the first time the book had been for sale. (I want to strongly emphasize that I do not think that most mental illnesses or even a majority of them are related to the demonic—that would be naive. However, it would also be naive to believe that it can never be related to the demonic.)

The mother had a copy of my book in her hand and opened it up to a chapter that dealt with curses and soul ties. She said, "I looked in the table of contents and saw this chapter. I thought, *That is where I should start reading.* Before I had read five pages, I realized I had done this sin and that I needed to repent. I took my Bible upstairs, put it on the bed, and knelt down to pray. I was weeping over my sin and then threw up." (I do not believe a person has to throw up to be delivered—I am just reporting her story.)

Within a few minutes, almost instantly, her daughter, who had been in bed and didn't want to get out of it, and who had also quit speaking in sentences, just yes and no, and little more, walked into the room where her mother was and said, "Mom, why are you crying? Are you sad? Isn't your brother coming home this week? Shouldn't we go to the store and get groceries to prepare for his coming?" Then again the mother said to me, "I have my daughter back."

The next morning, I met the daughter. I have since received about an inch-thick document that verifies her schizophrenia. And she is now, months later, still showing no signs of the illness.

HEALED OF BIPOLAR DISORDER

When I was starting the Vineyard Christian Fellowship in St. Louis, we began by meeting in our home. During the first months of starting the church, with fewer than ten people committed to us, I experienced my first breakthrough in regard to mental illness. A young man came to my home and asked if I would pray for him. We will call him Mac.

Mac was engaged to be married, but was worried about his battle with bipolar disorder. He had been married before, but he had divorced due to his battle with the condition. Every year now, for several years, he would end up in the mental ward of a hospital for one to two weeks, even though he was on medication. He would become delusional, and in the worst episodes, did things that were embarrassing, such as stripping naked and running down the street. At one point he had even gone to Oral Roberts University and stood up, calling Oral Roberts a false prophet. Mac didn't believe this about Oral Roberts when he was in his right mind, but in this delusional episode he had to be removed from the auditorium.

I took Mac up to the bedroom of our small townhouse to have a more private place to pray with him. I sat him on the bed, sat down beside him, placed my hands on his head in the temple area, and softly began to pray. I commanded the chemistry of his brain to come into normalcy, for the chemicals in the brain to be balanced perfectly. I prayed against these attacks and blessed his brain with peace. I prayed against delusionary episodes and for sound mental health.

Mac told me that he felt peace while I was praying and some heat in his head. He never had another episode. He had been spending at least one to two weeks per year in the mental ward of the hospital, but after this prayer he has never had to be hospitalized for bipolar disorder. He continued to take his medication, but it has been reduced.

Mac told me afterward that my prayer had been a very different prayer. I had not yelled at him or his condition; I had not become dramatic or emotional. I had not told him it was up to him to have enough faith for his healing. I had not told him that his condition and the reason he had not been healed was because of some secret sin in his life he needed to discover and confess. I had simply, quietly prayed, commanding the condition to be changed by changing the chemistry of the brain.

I offered that prayer for Mac in 1986, and as I said, he has not had to be hospitalized since.

He did marry, and he and his wife had several children. Shortly after their first child was born, Mac discovered that his wife had breast cancer and had to have a mastectomy. This was such a stressful situation that Mac thought it best to check himself in to the hospital, but after one day he realized that even under such stress he had not had an episode, so he checked himself out. Since this wasn't a situation where, due to a bipolar episode, a doctor had committed him, his stay was less than twenty-four hours and he was self-released.

Mac and his wife became the leaders of a specialty group at my church for those who had been diagnosed with some form of a mental illness. He faithfully led the group for years.

WOMAN SUFFERING SEVERE TRAUMA IS HEALED BY THE JOY OF THE LORD

Pastor D. was pastor of a church in the Spokane, Washington, area. His daughter had been traumatized by being raped. Thousands of dollars had been spent on professional counseling, but she was little better. Then, during a service, she was hit by the power of God. It was not a time where she was seeking healing or prayer for healing. The Holy Spirit came upon her, and she began to bend over at the waist, moving her head toward the floor, and she was laughing. After about twenty minutes of this bizarre behavior, the manifestation ended and she was healed from that moment of the emotional and psychological illness.

HEALED FROM DEPRESSION

On January 20, 1994, Carole Baerg was the first person healed in my meetings on the first night of the outbreak of the presence of God at the Toronto Vineyard. A series of meetings that lasted twelve-and-a-half years, six nights a week, at the same church became known as the Toronto Blessing. That night, I wasn't even praying for Carole to be healed. I had simply gone over to her and blessed her. She slid off her seat onto the floor and began laughing. As I walked away, I had an impression: *"Go back and tell her she has been sad too long."* I obeyed the impression, went back to her, made my hand like a pitcher with the thumb as the spout, and positioned it above her head and mouth. I told her, "God says you have been sad too long. Take another drink." Carole was hit with even more boisterous laughter, which lasted for some time that night.

About two weeks later, Carole was asked to share her testimony at a women's conference, but as soon as she tried to speak, she was overcome by the Holy Spirit. Then, others around her were overcome as well.

The following year Carole traveled to Belgium, and a woman came to her with a daughter who was almost nine months pregnant, but her child was dead, and she was instructed to wait another week to deliver the body. Carole prayed for this woman.

Three years later, she returned to Belgium, where a little boy ran up to her, declaring himself the "miracle baby" that she had prayed for.

As of two years ago, Carole was sixty-four years old and traveled regularly throughout Europe and the rest of the world. She reported to me a few years back, "Twenty years ago, I was ready to die, but now I am more full of life than ever."[6]

GIRL HEALED OF KIDNEY DISEASE

During a healing seminar I held at a Presbyterian church in Vienna, Illinois, just a few weeks after my wife and I had received an impartation and began to experience gifts of the Holy Spirit, my wife, DeAnne, had an amazing word of knowledge. She gave the word, "Kidney." There was a ten-year-old girl present who had a rare kidney disease. We prayed for her, and God healed her. We know she was healed because her parents brought her back to the meeting the next week, having had her examined by their doctor, who reported the kidney disease was gone.

On our way home on the night DeAnne had given the word of knowledge about the kidney, I asked her, "How did you get that word about the kidney? Did you feel it, think it, see it, read it, or say it?" (Those were the only ways we knew at that time that you could receive a word of knowledge; now we know two more ways—by experiencing it through an unusual experience for which God gives you the interpretation, and by dreaming it.) DeAnne answered, "I saw it." This really intrigued me, and I asked, "DeAnne, I know you; you don't have any knowledge of human anatomy. How did you know what you saw was a kidney?" She responded, "I didn't! When I saw it, I said, 'God, what is that?' And He answered, 'Kidney.'"

OPEN VISION WORD OF KNOWLEDGE
SAVES BOY FROM DEATH

About six months after the visitation at our Baptist church, my associate pastor, Tom Simpson, a coal miner, had left the Baptist church to help me plant the first Vineyard church in Illinois, one of the first east of Denver. During the Sunday morning service, he had an open vision. (An open vision is one of the seven ways a word of knowledge can occur. In it your field of vision is taken up with the vision God is giving you. It is not a mental picture, like a daydream.)

Tom did not understand how to interpret the vision he saw, so he didn't give the word during the worship service. That afternoon, the exact same vision occurred again while he was visiting with his extended family. During the evening service the exact same vision occurred for the third time. I was leading the service. He came to me quite shaken and shared the vision.

Three times Tom had seen a boy, about twelve years old, who was naked. His muscles on the left side of his body had atrophied, and as Tom continued to look at the boy in the vision, the muscles on his right side began to wither as well. Since we were starting a new church, Tom wondered if the picture was a metaphor representing the new church we were starting, and if so, if it meant it was going to wither and die. Tom told me, "I don't know how to interpret what I have seen, but I have seen it three times." So I addressed the congregation, asking, "Does this vision make sense to anyone?"

There was a visitor that evening from another church. I'll call her

Helen. This woman told us that she understood the vision. She said, "There is a boy about twelve years old who attends my church. He has a rare disease that is causing his muscles to atrophy. The muscles on his left side have already atrophied, and the doctors say that the disease is going to go to his right side. This is ultimately a terminal disease."

She continued, "However, his mother doesn't believe in you guys; she thinks you are a cult. She wouldn't bring him here for prayer. She does, however, believe in prayer. I know her well. I believe we should call her."

I stopped the worship service, and Tom and I, Helen, and a couple of others gathered around for the call. When we reached the mother, Helen explained what was happening. We prayed over the phone for Ryan, her son. Helen asked his mother to put her hands on Ryan and join us in the prayer.

Ryan was already scheduled to go to St. Louis the next day, to Shriners Hospital to be rechecked. When the doctor examined Ryan, he told the family that the rare disease was gone, his right side had not been affected, and his left side was regaining muscle strength. Ryan had received quite a miraculous healing.

A WORD OF KNOWLEDGE BRINGS HEALING

I was in Uberlandia, Brazil, ministering at a large church of several thousand members. I had a dream one night, and the next morning, while ministering healing, I remembered it. I wasn't sure this was a real word of knowledge, so I saved the word of knowledge for last, in case it was not God. I said, "Last night I had a dream. In this dream I saw two hands. There were no arms or body, just the two hands. And on the palms, close to the thumbs, something was sticking out about an inch or two, and it was about three inches wide."

Immediately a man on the back row jumped up and came to the

front of the church. His hands were held open, and I could see large scars in the palms of one of his hands. He came to me, placed his hand in mine, and before I could say, "Come, Holy Spirit" he was already healed. He told me he knew he was going to be healed because what I described was exactly what happened to him. In a freak accident that severed his arteries and nerves, a large sliver of wood had gone into his hand, and it stuck out about one to two inches. His hand had been paralyzed, and he couldn't move it. But on this night he was instantly healed.

OSCAR IN SINGAPORE GETS A NEW LEASE ON LIFE

I was one of the speakers at a gathering in Singapore of probably eight to ten thousand people. Bill Johnson and Heidi Baker were the other two main speakers. After one service, due to jet lag, I woke up at about 3:00 a.m. in my hotel room, and was unable to go back to sleep. Lying in bed, I asked the Lord to give me words of knowledge, and especially to give me some name. During the next minutes I heard two or three names of people, along with several names of places and five or six physical conditions. I wrote them down on a small, pink piece of paper, like a sticky note.

The next day, during the ministry time, I called the Global Awakening ministry team that had joined us from many countries for this trip. They began to give words of knowledge. One of the words of knowledge was "trouble swallowing." A few minutes later, two young women who were quite ecstatic were brought to the stage. When they heard the words "trouble swallowing," they called a Buddhist mother whose two-and-a-half-year-old son couldn't swallow. He had no swallowing reflexes and had been fed through a tube his whole life. The young women had prayed for the boy, and he was healed.

As they were telling the story in Chinese, I heard the name Oscar. When they retold the story in English, when I heard "Oscar," I became very excited, I looked down at my piece of paper and saw where I had written Oscar the night before. I had also written down "trouble swallowing." But I didn't know the two were connected. When I showed the two young women the paper where I had written the name Oscar, they began to jump up and down, screaming, on the stage and hugged me.[7]

The following year, I was back again in Singapore, ministering again. This time during the invitation to accept Jesus Christ as Savior, Oscar's mother and father renounced Buddhism and accepted Jesus.

• • •

Isaiah 53:5 tells us that "by [Jesus] wounds we are healed." That wasn't a word for that time and place only. God's Word is as true today as it was when the prophet penned those words. Healing is for me, and it's for you—today.

CHAPTER 4

THE DEAF HEAR

E ars that hear and eyes that see—the LORD has made them both," we read in Proverbs 20:12. To me, this is proof positive that God's intention is and always has been that every person should be able to hear. Furthermore, it was part of Jesus' self-understanding of His commission from the Father (Luke 4:18). Jesus told His disciples, "As the Father has sent me, I am sending you" (John 20:21). And again, in the Great Commission of Matthew 28:18–20, we see that newly baptized disciples are to be taught to obey everything Jesus taught His disciples to do. There is none whom the Lord wants to remain deaf—no matter what theology you have been taught.

This chapter focuses on the healing of the deaf. In my years of ministry, I have seen many whose ears, once closed, were opened. Here are only a few of their stories.

A CREATIVE MIRACLE IN THE UKRAINE

One of the most memorable nights I have experienced occurred in Odessa, Ukraine. I was praying for a twelve- to fourteen-year-old boy who was deaf in one ear. I commanded his ear to open and for him to hear. When I reinterviewed him, I found out he had been healed the first time I prayed.

The mother was ecstatic about her son's healing. She even reprimanded me for not being excited enough. I told her, "I *am* excited. I am happy for your son, but I have seen other people who were deaf get their hearing. This is not my first time to see someone deaf healed." Then his mother said to me, "But have you ever seen someone healed of deafness who didn't have an auditory nerve?" I was shocked. I realized a creative miracle had just happened. I joined the mother in exuberant celebration of the miracle.

Later, I asked her how they knew there was no auditory nerve. She replied, "We took him to a specialist in Odessa, and then to another one in Venice, Italy. Both doctors confirmed his auditory nerve had been destroyed, that he didn't have an auditory nerve."

EIGHT HEALED BY RAIN FROM HEAVEN

In September 2001 we were in Brazil at a very large church. I have already spoken about this church in Manaus, Brazil, in the rain forest. We had a smaller team of about thirty to forty on the Global International ministry team. (This was when I was just beginning to learn about the angelic realm, and their role in the healing ministry.)

I was preaching. During the sermon I said something to the effect, "God, let the river of Ezekiel 47 and Revelation 21 run through this place, and whoever the river touches, heal them." Seconds after I said these words, there was a clap of thunder, and it began to pour. It was the dry season, when for several weeks it usually does not rain. The building we were in had only the concrete floor, the pillars, the restrooms, and the roof completed. There were no walls, and there were no gutters. On my left sat about forty people in the deaf section, which was located next to what would have been a wall, if they'd had one.

The wind came and blew the rain in on the deaf section. In just a few minutes we heard people yelling. They were so excited. Eight of the deaf persons had been healed when the rain came upon them. They were soaked by the rain. It was a God thing. No one had been praying for them. The rain was like the mist you might see at a theme park on a hot summer day, to cool things off. This mist could be seen floating across the ten-thousand-seat auditorium. Then, as it began to fall on the people, more healings sovereignly broke out.

I turned to my pastor friend, Tom Hauser, who had been power-fully touched another time in Brazil and had received his own power-ful impartation, and said, "Tom, I have lost the meeting; God has taken over." Before long we had eight of the deaf persons up on the platform. They could hear and were letting us know what they were hearing, which side, and how many hand claps. Though they could not speak, having never heard words, they were trying to learn to speak. It was one of the most amazing nights of my life.

Another time, at this same church, Gary saw an angel while he was teaching, and fell over in the Spirit. I asked his wife to go onstage to take over. She began to prophesy to the wind that was blowing in the building, which now had walls. The wind started blowing so hard it blew over the back rows of chairs and a large door on the stage. Men ran outside to find that there was no wind blowing outside the building, only on the inside. Healings broke out during this time.

On the same trip Gary told me he had seen "warrior angels" in the crowd that night that were clearing out the demonic and opening heaven. Later during my time of ministry, he told me he saw hundreds of healing angels come in on my right. I announced that a lot of healing was about to break out on the right side of the building, but did not mention angels. That night, almost ten thousand people were healed. This was by far the most healings, and it was the only night of eight where there was angelic activity on this particular trip.

EIGHT DAYS, ONE CHURCH, SIXTY DEAF PERSONS HEALED

The next time we went to this same church, we had sixty deaf people healed during that week. This was the same service in which the man who had been shot and whose spinal cord was severed, was healed and got out of his wheelchair.[1] In addition there were ten tumors that disappeared in the same church. There were also fifteen blind people healed.

DEAF COUPLE HEALED AND BEGIN SIGNING FOR THE DEAF COMMUNITY

Moving from the north to the south in Brazil to Uberlandia, in another church where our teams have seen many miracles and hundreds of healings, we experienced more healings of deafness. (It was at this church, as well as in Mozambique, where a team of research scientists were testing for healing of deafness or partial deafness. They had bought several thousand dollars' worth of equipment to test for hearing. The team had received a grant from the John Templeton Fund for research.[2]

Time will not allow for telling all the stories of the number of deaf people healed at this church or the numbers of deaf ears opened; sometimes people are only deaf in one ear, so technically they're not deaf. I want to tell the story of one couple who were part of the rather large deaf community of this large church that numbered in the thousands.

On this Global Awakening International Ministry trip, I had three young interns I was mentoring: Timothy Berry, Chris Ishak, and Annie Byrne. Timothy, in his early twenties at the time, was involved in praying for the husband in this deaf marriage. He had been able to hear as a younger man, but had lost his hearing completely by this time. But since he could hear when he was younger, he could understand speech. God healed him that night.

The next day, this same man was signing for the deaf section. The next year when we returned to this church, his wife received her hearing through prayer. (Having never spoken, she has had to learn to speak.)

EARDRUM AND EAR BONES CREATED

I don't want you to get the idea that only in far-off countries do we see healing, including the healing of deaf ears. It happens in America too. One of the more recent healings of a deaf ear occurred in Redding, California, at Bethel Church, which was meeting at the civic auditorium for a healing conference. For one woman, disease had destroyed not only the eardrum, but also all the bones in her left ear. But on this day, her hearing was restored. I do not know how the woman was healed or who prayed for her. She simply came up to give her testimony. This is what she said:

> I had a disease in my ear. It is called cholesteatoma. It ate away the ear bones and eardrum in my left ear. I could only hear very loud noises, but I couldn't hear the TV or talk on the phone. This weekend, that changed, and I think I can hear out of my ear just fine. I can hear tiny noises, like rubbing my fingers together in this ear, which is a total change.

HEALED BY A GLORY CLOUD

About fifteen years ago, I took four young interns with me to Raleigh, North Carolina. I was speaking on the manifestations I was seeing in Brazil when, in the middle of the sermon, a woman stood up and yelled, "Do you see it?" Immediately I saw people with the look of astonishment on their faces. Three of my interns, Will Hart, Jamie Galloway, and Brandon Sundberg, who were seated on the front row in front of me, instantly threw themselves to the floor, faces down.

I was on the stage, with bright lights shining in my eyes, which made it impossible for me to see what others were seeing. I came down from the stage so I could see. I saw a translucent cloud that looked like the heat waves rising from the fields on a hot summer day. Inside the cloud, which started at the ceiling and came down to the level of my knees and was about three feet in diameter, were small silver, gold, red, blue, and green particles spinning like a multilevel milky way. Some of the particles seemed to be lighting up. I tried to touch one, but they would move away from my finger every time.

As I stood in the cloud, I felt this amazing peace. A sense of *all is well.* I don't remember how long I stood in the cloud, but I later stepped out to continue leading the service. We went back into worship and then prayed for healing. There were twice as many people healed on the side of the building where the cloud was manifesting. People began to move from one side of the building to the side the cloud was on.

Then an older man who had fought in the Korean War spoke out to the pastor. "Pastor John, I can hear! I haven't been able to hear since the Korean War—that's why I often fall asleep during your sermons—I can't hear you." This man had been seated right in front of the cloud. No one had prayed for him. He had been sovereignly healed because of his proximity to the cloud.

The cloud remained through the worship, the prayer for healing, and the continuation of the sermon. It remained for about two hours, then dissipated.

Later, I was told by the pastor that over the next ten years, the cloud appeared two other times in the sanctuary.

• • •

So now we have seen that today, as always, God still heals the sick, the lame, the blind, the deaf. But does He still raise the dead? Or was that a miracle relegated only to Jesus' time, and reserved for the likes of Lazarus, Jairus's daughter, and Dorcas? Let's find out.

CHAPTER 5

THE DEAD ARE RAISED

In the New Testament Jesus raised Jairus's daughter. He raised Lazarus. And, John tells us that if everything Jesus had done had been written, all the books of the world couldn't contain the stories. Obviously, this is hyperbole, used to emphasize that only a small fraction of all the healings and miracles Jesus did have been recorded in the Gospels. In the book of Acts, Peter raised Dorcas from the dead, and Paul raised the young man who fell from the window. But resurrections are taking place today too—in this day and age, and from the history of the church there are many testimonies of people being raised from the dead. I want to share some of the contemporary stories of the dead raising with you. I also want to point out that they have been used to bring whole provinces that were almost totally non-Christian to Christ.

STORIES FROM AROUND THE WORLD

In the opening chapter of his 2005 book, *Mega Shift* (Colorado Springs: Empowerment House, 2005), James Rutz shares several stories of people being raised from the dead. The first involves a forty-year-old Buddhist monk from Myanmar, named Athet Pyan Shintaw Paulu. He was dead for three days in 1998, but at his funeral, just before being cremated, he sat up in his coffin before a crowd of hundreds and shouted:

It's all a lie! I saw our ancestors burning and being tortured in some kind of fire. I also saw Buddha and many other Buddhist holy men. They were all in a sea of fire! . . . We must listen to the Christians. They're the only ones who know the truth.

This man had never read a Bible and hadn't heard of hell, and so his experience was a traumatic shock. He saw people from the Bible, like Goliath, whom he described as a nine-foot-plus-tall man in military armor, with a wound in his forehead.

Paulu's testimony is heard today on a widely circulated cassette. It is now a serious crime in Myanmar to be caught with a copy of that tape.[1]

Another account in *Mega Shift* comes from Seoul, Korea, where in 1974, the five-year-old son of Pastor David Yonggi Cho died from eating contaminated food. The pastor was called in from an elders' meeting and even after hours of praying for his son, watched him slowly fade away and die. But even after watching his boy become cold and stiff, he would not give up. He told the Lord that he would not leave the room until He gave his son back.[2]

After praying and praising until after midnight, he shouted his son's name, saying, "Samuel, in the name of Jesus Christ of Nazareth, stand up and walk!" His son sprang to his feet!

Later, he told his father what he had seen and experienced in heaven. He spoke of seeing Jesus and members of Cho's church who had died. Jesus then told Samuel that He couldn't keep him because his father wouldn't let him go.[3]

• • •

Here's a story from Mexico after an outbreak of black measles killed about forty people in the village of Chiconamiel in 1998. A widow who had recently become a Christian lost both of her teenage daughters and, by then, had to drag their bodies to the graveyard herself, as there were no helpers left alive. And there were twenty-one others ahead of her, with only two gravediggers who had strength to work. Because of the heat, she sprinkled lime powder on the girls' bodies as a disinfectant and walked home. It took eight hours to reach the home of her Christian contacts, where she went seeking prayer.

Because it was nightfall, her friends waited for morning before setting off for the village. But the time they reached the cemetery, it was again approaching evening. The line had shortened, so they surrounded the girls' bodies, praying in the authority of the Lord Jesus Christ. They called the girls by name, and they both sat up.[4]

• • •

The next account is a lengthier one, and the events took place in Onitsha, Nigeria, in November 2001. On Thursday, November 29, Pastor Daniel Ekechukwu and his wife, Nneka, had a misunderstanding that degenerated into an argument that ended in her slapping him. He was very offended by this incident, to the point of not even acknowledging her attempt to reconcile the next morning. Pastor Daniel admitted that throughout the day, November 30, he angrily thought about how he would put his wife in her place when he returned home.

He would not, however, make it home that Friday.

As he was driving home that evening, the brakes on his twenty-year-old Mercedes 230E failed as he was heading down a steep hill, and his car crashed into a concrete pillar that was built to prevent cars from going over a steep embankment. He was not wearing a seatbelt (few Nigerians did in 2001; that changed in 2003, when wearing a seatbelt become a national law), and his chest hit forcibly against the steering wheel, apparently damaging to his internal organs, as he was soon vomiting up blood and having difficulty breathing. Little did he know that soon he would lose all signs of life.

Daniel was not able to remove himself from his car, but frantic onlookers pulled him out. One bystander volunteered her car while another offered to drive him to St. Charles Borromeo Hospital, not far away, on the outskirts of Onitsha.

Within minutes of their arrival at the hospital, a doctor began administering emergency treatment, but Daniel knew his body was not responding to it. He began praying the prayer of a man who knows he is going to die, asking God to forgive him of all his sins so that he would be ready to stand before the Lord. He also sent for his wife, Nneka, with whom he had refused to speak when he left his home earlier that day. She fainted upon hearing the news of her husband's accident and condition, but when revived, was taken by a Christian neighbor to the hospital. Daniel's friend (whom I interviewed at length) was with her and essentially witnessed everything that transpired during the next three days.

Upon seeing Daniel in critical condition when she arrived at St. Charles Borromeo Hospital, Daniel's wife burst into tears, begging her husband not to die and leave her. The doctor admitted that there was nothing he could do to save Daniel's life (keep in mind this was a third-world hospital), so Daniel requested that he be transferred by ambulance to Umezuruike Hospital at Owerri, where his personal doctor practiced. That hospital was eighty kilometers away. Daniel's wife arranged for the ambulance, against the advice of doctors at St. Charles Hospital. It was on the way to Umezuruike Hospital that Daniel died.

Daniel was lying in the back of the ambulance while his wife was in the front passenger seat. He began to feel that he was not going to survive, so he called for his wife to come to him. He said his good-byes, gave her instructions about certain church and personal documents, and admonished her to take care of their sons and his church. She began sobbing and amid her tears, strongly rebuked him for such negative statements. He was a man of God, she reminded him, and should have faith and not be speaking of dying!

As she was speaking, Daniel saw two large angels (they were so large that he later wondered how they fit inside the ambulance—one was as big as the ambulance) who were completely white, even the pupils of their eyes. Daniel tried to speak to the angels, but one held his finger to his lips, motioning for his silence. The angels lifted him on either side, and Daniel realized that there were now two of him. The angels were holding him under each arm of his spirit man (which was perfectly whole), while his broken body lay below. Once they left the ambulance, Daniel became oblivious to the natural world.

When the ambulance arrived at Umezuruike Hospital with Daniel's body, it was now late at night, and Daniel's doctor was not there. A member of the medical staff, however, examined his body and sadly told Nneka that her husband was dead and there was nothing that could be done. Nneka refused to believe the bad report.

So they drove to the Federal Medical Center in Owerri, but found no doctor there either. Finally they drove to the Eunice Clinic, and there Daniel was confirmed dead by Dr. Jossy Anuebunwa. There was no breathing, no heartbeat or pulse, and Daniel's pupils were dilated and fixed. The doctor said that there was nothing he could do. A death certificate was issued at 11:30 p.m., November 30, 2001.

They then drove Daniel's corpse to his father's house in a nearby village, and naturally Daniel's father and other family members were heartbroken at the sight of Daniel's dead body and wept profusely. Daniel's father instructed them to take his body to Ikeduru General Hospital Mortuary (now known as Inyishi Community Hospital Mortuary) not far away. They arrived there around one o'clock on Saturday morning. The resident mortician, Mr. Barlington Manu, received the corpse, and the family members departed.

The primitive Nigerian mortuary where Daniel's body was taken had no cold storage facilities, so the mortician injected embalming chemicals into Daniel's fingers and into his feet. He then prepared to embalm Daniel's body fully by cutting Daniel's inner thigh in order to insert a tube by which he could inject more embalming fluid. As he did this, he experienced a shock that pushed him away from the corpse. This did not surprise him, as he had experienced similar forces before and attributed them to occult powers. (Such things are *widely* believed in Africa and highly respected by all African pastors whom I know. Africans never understand the skepticism of Americans regarding the reality of occult power.)

After a second attempt and a second shock that somewhat paralyzed his right arm, he concluded that Daniel must have been a member of a powerful secret society. He assumed, however, that after some occult sacrifices and incantations, the powers in the corpse would subside, and he could then complete his work. (This mortician, of course, was not a Christian, but converted after Daniel's resurrection.) So he instructed an assistant to lay Daniel's body in the rear of the mortuary, where many other corpses were already laid. (Incidentally, Daniel said that people could smell the embalming chemicals coming out of his body for two weeks after his resurrection. They would hug him and hold their noses.)

Around two o'clock Saturday morning, the mortician, who lived very close to the mortuary, was disturbed by songs of worship coming from inside his mortuary, which stopped as soon as he approached the mortuary doorway. This occurred twice. Upon searching for the music's source in his mortuary, he noticed some kind of light emanating from the face of Daniel's corpse. This completely unnerved him.

The mortician was so disturbed that he located Daniel's father on Saturday morning to inform him of what had been happening and to request that he remove Daniel's corpse from his mortuary.

Then, on Saturday night, while she was sleeping, Daniel's wife experienced a dream in which she saw her husband's face, and he was asking her why they had left him in the mortuary. He stated that he was not dead and that she should take him to Onitsha, where German evangelist Reinhard Bonnke was preaching. She determined to do so, even though her family thought she was out of her mind. Daniel had been dead for more than twenty-eight hours.

The family finally yielded, but purchased a casket and brought funeral clothing for the mortician to dress Daniel. Rigor mortis had fully set in by this time. An ambulance was hired on Sunday morning, December 2, and the casket that contained Daniel's body was taken to Grace of God Mission (a large church) in Onitsha, about one and half hours away, where Reinhard Bonnke was preaching at an afternoon church dedication service. They arrived at the church around one in the afternoon.

The church grounds were being protected by swarms of federal, state, and local security guards for the sake of Bonnke, who had received many death threats and was hated by Muslims all over Africa. (Not to mention that the World Trade Center had been destroyed by Muslim hijackers just weeks before.) For this reason, the security guards would not allow Daniel's casket to be brought onto church grounds, thinking it might actually contain explosives. Daniel's wife loudly pleaded with them, and opened the casket to show them her dead husband, which resulted in their mocking and even flogging her because of her persistence. She caused such a disturbance that the senior pastor was notified, and his son instructed that Daniel's wife be permitted to bring his body to the church without the casket, and that it be placed in the basement. Daniel's body was laid there on two tables pushed together in a Sunday school room.

Some believers gathered around Daniel's body and prayed while

Reverend Bonnke, who knew nothing of the dead body in the basement, preached and prayed. Eventually, someone noticed that Daniel's corpse twitched, and then irregular breathing started. By this time, Bonnke had left the premises entirely.

The attendant believers began praying fervently, and because Daniel's body was stiff and cold, they began massaging his neck, arms, and legs. When those in the sanctuary got word that a dead man below was coming back to life, the basement room was soon jammed with people. Suddenly Daniel sneezed and arose with a jump. It was somewhere between 3:50 and 5:15 p.m. on Sunday afternoon. Daniel had died Friday night around ten o'clock. He slowly became fully coherent over the next few hours.[5]

It's extremely encouraging to us that these accounts continue to increase in number and there are now hundreds from which to choose.

• • •

One final account from *Mega Shift* comes again from Mexico. A twenty-year-old believer had died after a massive seizure in Chilengo, and a handful of Christians gathered to pray for her. Ladies from the town decorated her body with flowers while the men prayed in another part of the room.

One of the men went outside to relieve himself and encountered a large, evil-looking black man and a big, black dog. There are no black people in that area, so the man's skin color had no racial meaning for him, but the man's evil expression did scare him, so he ran back inside for help. Another of the men came out and shouted, "In the name of Jesus Christ, leave!" The dog ran off into the woods, followed by his master. Somewhat shaken, the men went back inside, only to find the girl sitting up, brushing the flowers from her body. They realized then that what they had seen was a manifestation of a spirit of death.[6]

RESURRECTIONS IN THE UNITED STATES

A woman named Nancy and her husband told me about their grandson who was raised from the dead. It was summer, and the family was at a picnic at a lake. The grandson was out on the lake, riding a Jet Ski. There was a terrible accident involving a collision, and the boy was killed instantly.

Quickly they rushed to a boat and made their way to the scene of the accident. This took several minutes. They found the boy floating in the water, dead. They brought him into the boat and came back to shore. A doctor who was present examined their grandson and told the family that he was dead.

Nancy began to pray for her grandson. She called him by name, commanding him to come back to life. For several minutes she spoke life into him and called upon his spirit to come back into his body. Finally, with no sign of life and perhaps as many as fifteen to twenty minutes having elapsed since the accident, Nancy yelled, "Johnny, this is your grandmother, and I command you to come back into your body."

Suddenly he came back to life. And even though he was without oxygen many minutes past the time when brain damage should have occurred, there was no brain damage at all.

The young man graduated from college this year.

FIVE-YEAR-OLD BOY, BACK FROM THE DEAD

Back in the 1990s, I was preaching for a great pastor, Cleddie Keith, at an Assemblies of God church in Florence, Kentucky. I was preparing to preach the sermon "A Biblical Basis for Healing." As I was going over the many texts involved in this sermon, I came to Matthew 10:7–8: "As you go, proclaim this message: 'The kingdom of heaven has come near.' Heal the sick, raise the dead, cleanse those who have leprosy, drive out demons."

I was struggling with this passage. The Holy Spirit spoke to me and said, *"You don't like that last verse, do you?"* I responded, "No, Lord, I don't like that verse. We are trying to get the sick healed, and You're telling us to raise the dead. This verse is an embarrassment to the church."

At this time, I only knew of two resurrection stories outside of the Bible. Unlike today, when there are hundreds of stories of resurrections happening in the world—then I only knew of two. I had not met Heidi Baker yet, so I hadn't heard of the resurrections occurring through the bush pastors in the Iris churches.

The Holy Spirit by strong impression spoke to me again, *"Don't you dare become an experience-based preacher who will only preach what he has experienced. Don't you dare lower My Word (the Bible) to the level of your experience! You preach My Word, and let your experience rise to it, but don't bring it down to your experience!"*

That afternoon I preached this message for the first time, and when it came to the resurrection, I told the two stories that I had heard from Omar Cabrera Sr. about how he raised his son from death, and how he raised a friend's wife from the dead. This is what happened to her.

Omar was driving, along with his wife and another couple, through the mountains when he hit a boulder that had fallen on the road, causing his car to careen off the road into a lake. The car sank in the water rather quickly. Omar was able to get out and swam to get his wife out. When they reached the top of the water to get their breath, he saw his friend, one of his pastors, but they did not see his wife. Together they dived back into the murky water to reach the car, looking for the pastor's wife. They found her in the backseat, which by now had filled up with water. She wasn't breathing. They quickly brought her to the surface and carried her out to the bank. She had drowned; there was no pulse.

They tried to revive her using the normal means of rolling her on her side and compressing the chest. However, it was to no avail. Then, having no experience in praying for a dead person to live, Omar began to call her by name and call her spirit back into her body.

About fifteen to twenty minutes had passed since the car had fallen into the lake, when suddenly, she gasped as her spirit came back into her body. Shortly, they were picked up by another car and driven to the hospital, where they could better check on the woman. The hospital didn't even keep her overnight; they released her, with no brain damage.

Afterward, I felt the Lord was telling me that we wouldn't see dead raisings unless we preached and taught about them. I remember saying in my sermon in Kentucky, "We never know when we may be called upon to pray for someone who has died, but believe it was not time for them to die. So, I am telling you everything I know about dead raising."

A few years later, I met two men who had been there when I preached on raising the dead. They had been on the worship team. They were in their twenties, and one of them was the electric guitar player. He told me how his son had been raised from the dead.

The boy's mother had dreamed the night before that there was a death in the family. She assumed it to be one of the elderly family members. She had prayed against the dream, believing it could be a warning.

Her husband was walking through the home, and as he passed the window, he noticed people standing out in the road and in his yard. He quickly ran out of the house, with a great sense of dread, because he had not noticed his five-year-old son in the room. Going out the door, he saw his son's tricycle bent, lying in the yard. He ran toward the street, only to see his worst nightmare. His little son had been hit by a car and was lying in the street, with people gathered around him.

The father had recently completed training as an emergency medical technician for his ambulance job. He had been trained in how to recognize death. His son had all the signs of death. When the boy's mother saw what had happened, she began to scream and cry. Someone had already called 911 for an ambulance. The man placed his hands on his son and was filled with horror and grief.

Then he remembered the teaching I had given a short few weeks before. He began to call out his son's name, commanding his spirit to come back into his body.

After a few minutes his son gasped and began to scream with pain. What a wonderful sound to this father—the cry of pain instead of the silence of death.

When the 911 attendants arrived, they realized the boy would have to be medevaced by helicopter to another hospital due to the seriousness of his injuries, especially the multiple breaks in his bones.

A couple of weeks later, when the parents saw the doctor, they asked if the body cast he was wearing could be cut down about an inch from the top because of the discomfort their son was experiencing. The doctor told them, "That is impossible; your son's injuries are such that it will take many weeks for his bones to heal. We are just X-raying him to see if the bones are beginning to mend correctly."

Several minutes later, the doctor came out and told the parents, "I have never seen this before—I don't understand how it is possible—but your son's bones have already completely healed, and we are cutting the cast off."

I believe the same resurrection power that brought him back to life was also powerfully effective in healing his bones weeks before they should have normally healed.

DR. CRANDALL'S STORY

On the morning of September 20, 2006, a man drove himself to the hospital. Once he had arrived, he collapsed. Dr. Crandall was working that day at the hospital, and because he was the cardiologist on-staff that day, he attended to the man. The team fought to keep the man alive, but there was no response. Dr. Crandall did everything possible, then called the time of death.

The nurse prepared the man's body for the morgue, and Dr. Crandall finished his chart notes and walked out the door. But then he heard a voice say, *"Pray for that man."* He thought it would be no use, but the voice came back again and told him to pray for the man. Dr. Crandall decided to honor the Lord, so he came back in and walked to the side of the body.

The nurse was still there, and Dr. Crandall stood next to the dead body, opened his mouth, and said, "Father God, I cry out for this man's soul. If he does not know You as his Lord and Savior, Father, raise him from the dead now, in Jesus' name."

Another doctor walked in just then, and Dr. Crandall said, "Shock this man one more time." That doctor, out of respect for Dr. Crandall, went to the body with the defibrillator paddles and shocked the man. Instantly, his heartbeat came back, perfect and regular, which I've never seen before. The nurse screamed, "What have you done?"

The man started moving and breathing; then the fingers started twitching. The man was immediately moved to ICU and woke up three days later with no evidence of brain or organ damage. When Dr. Crandall came in the next week, the man was sitting up in bed.

Dr. Crandall asked where he had been when he was dead, and the man said he was in darkness, alone and disappointed. Dr. Crandall asked the man if he was ready to accept God into his heart, and he did. He is now back at work and has no lasting complications from his death.[7]

=D TO LIFE IN BRAZIL

, I became friends with an amazing pastor. This
church in the city to more than fifty thousand people
in their cell groups. He also moved from Santarem to
eleza, Brazil, where in eight years he saw the church and churches
he started in this other state grow to more than thirty thousand
people. He is a man of utmost integrity and one of the most respected
spiritual leaders in the nation of Brazil.

During one of my first trips to Santarem, I spoke about raising the
dead. Unlike the story in Kentucky, where I was embarrassed to talk
about raising the dead, by this time I had met and interviewed people
who had been raised from the dead (most of these interviews occurred
in Mozambique), along with those who had prayed for them to be
raised from the dead and had witnessed the power such resurrections
had on the villages where they occurred. The most common result
was the coming of many to faith in Jesus and commitment to become
a Christian disciple.

Encouraged by my personal knowledge of the dead being raised,
I shared with many pastors and leaders in Santarem, Brazil. I also had
an impartation service where many of the leaders and pastors were
touched mightily by the power of God. One such pastor–church
planter left the meeting renewed in the power of God and the faith
of God. On one of my return trips to visit, he told me this story.

He was going through the Amazon River basin, sharing about
the power of the gospel, and was praying for the sick. In one of his
meetings, he prayed for the people to be touched by the power of God,
just as I had prayed for the leaders in Santarem. One of the men there
was powerfully touched by the Holy Spirit.

Shortly afterward, the man's son, who was in his late teens, died
in his house. Having heard the church planter repeat the stories I had

told, the man prayed for his son to be raised from the dead. For more than *twelve hours*, this father prayed for his son to be restored to life.

BRAZILIAN GIRLS RAISED FROM THE DEAD

Earlier I mentioned Uberlandia, a city in southern Brazil. As I said, I have been there several times to minister in a large church of multiple thousands. On one of the later trips, we had a miracle service where hundreds were healed. There we learned of two raisings from the dead. The first story was well-known by the thousands in this church because it happened right in front of the church.

Eight weeks earlier, a young girl, about twelve, was crossing the busy street in front of the church. Her mother was following a few steps behind her. The girl dropped a lead pencil and bent over to pick it up. Immediately she was hit by a motorcycle, and her body was thrown forward, her head hitting the concrete curb. The blow was so violent that her skull was cracked and her brain was exposed.

Her mother, who witnessed this horrible sight, ran to her daughter, who had died instantly. The mother began to cry out to God to restore her daughter to life.

Soon an ambulance was on the scene, as well as a vehicle from the fire department. These trained medical professionals told the mother her daughter was dead, that there was nothing she could do for her, and that it was too late to pray—she was gone.

The mother would not listen; instead, she persevered in her crying out to God for a miracle, for her daughter to be brought back to life. More than twenty minutes went by, and the paramedics and the fire department were becoming frustrated with the mother, insisting that she stop praying and allow them to take her daughter's body to the morgue.

The mother pulled out her phone and called the leader of her cell group and requested that she come to help pray for her daughter. The cell leader told her she would come immediately. When she arrived, she, too, placed her hands on her friend's dead daughter and joined in prayer for her resurrection. They prayed several more minutes, bringing the time since the accident to about thirty minutes.

Suddenly, the girl's spirit returned into her body and she came back to life!

The girl had to be taken to the hospital due to her cracked skull and exposed brain, in addition to a broken arm and damage to her leg, but she survived.

Eight weeks later, the girl came to our meeting at the church. Her arm was in a cast, she was seeing double, and she was in a wheelchair. But during the service, she was healed. She walked out of the wheelchair, the double vision cleared up, and the injury to her head closed even more.

When we interviewed her, we heard the story of her death and resurrection. She also told us that when she was hit by the motorcycle, "everything suddenly went black. Then," she said, "I was in this bright place, heaven. It was beautiful and it felt wonderful. Then Jesus came to me and told me I had to go back, that my mother and her friend wouldn't give up. I came back into my body and I was in pain."[8]

During this same series of meetings at the church in Uberlandia, we found out about another resurrection of a little girl.

On this night, the little girl, who was crippled, was on the stage, where some of my team were praying for people, when a train engineer on my team felt God lead him to ask the mother if it was okay to take the braces off the girl's legs. She had never been able to walk without them, because her heels couldn't touch the ground and her feet were malformed. But the mother agreed, and when they asked the child to walk, she did! And not only was she walking all over the stage; she was walking fast. Then the mother came to me to tell me the rest of the story.

On one of my first visits to the church, she said, she had come to me with a picture of her daughter on her smartphone. This is a custom that is quite common in Brazil, to bring pictures of one's family or loved ones who are in need of prayer for healing to the pastors or evangelists. (I personally never liked this practice, thinking there were more than enough people to pray for who were at the meeting, without taking time to pray for pictures.)

The mother went on to tell me that when she'd brought the picture of her baby, who was in the hospital, what she hadn't told me at the time was that the baby had died. I'd prayed—but not really with a gift of faith or even any faith, because I didn't have much expectancy for this smartphone prayer practice. When the mother returned to the hospital, however, her baby had returned to life and the monitor showed the heartbeat. The same little girl who'd just had her braces removed and was healed, had been raised from the dead just a few years earlier.

ONE LAST STORY

In another city in southern Brazil, I met a man who was a former prison warden. He told me his amazing story.

"The first time I met you," he said, "you prayed for me. I fell to the floor under the power of God and wept." I told him I believed God had knocked him down, that he was such a big, strong man that no mere man would have knocked him down. He was built like the Hulk.

"I returned home and to my job as overseer of the prison," he continued. "but I had received an anointing for healing at your meeting. I prayed for more than two hundred prisoners who received healing in one year.

"Then there was a riot, during which one of my guards was shot in the chest several times. I went to the hospital to pray for him. When

I arrived, I could see that the heart monitor indicated he had died. I didn't know how to pray for someone who had died. I'd had faith before I saw he was dead, but once I realized he was dead, I didn't have faith for him to be raised. But the man's wife saw me as I turned to leave. She sent someone outside the room to get me to come and pray for her husband to be raised from the dead. I didn't know what to do. I was very scared. But I came up to her husband, placed my hand upon his chest, and commanded him to come back to life. He did! I saw the heart monitor begin to beep again."

Then he told me, "I lost my job as the prison overseer, and became just a prison guard. I got a demotion from man but a promotion from God. He has called me to become a pastor, and I now have a church."

His sister didn't believe his story about raising the dead. But then her son was killed in an accident. He told me, "My sister called me and said, 'You healed that guard. Well, this is your nephew; come and pray for him to be raised from the dead.'"

He did, and the nephew was restored.

RESURRECTION MIRACLES IN MOZAMBIQUE

Supresa Sithole is one of the leaders of Iris Global, with Rolland and Heidi Baker. He has seen more than a hundred people raised from the dead. One of his accounts involves a person raised from the dead during a doctor's strike.

"We had gone to the hospital, but it was chaos in there [because of the strike]. We saw a woman lying down with open eyes and open mouth, covered in day-old worms. We started praying for [her], and after a while, I was thinking, *I needed to tell the doctor to remove her body from the hospital.* As I went to turn around, the woman coughed, the worms came out of her mouth, and she rose from the dead."[9]

Another testimony involves a dead baby that was brought to

Supresa for prayer. The baby was dried up, and Supresa wondered what had been wrong with the baby. He immediately began praying for God to raise the baby to life. "God," he said, "send your Holy Spirit with healing power."

All of a sudden, he could feel pain, and breath came to the baby. As soon as the baby started breathing, Supresa started to pray more, calling on the name of Jesus. The baby opened its eyes, was healed by the grace of God, and was raised from the dead.

After that, the mother brought another dead baby to Supresa, saying, "I am bringing you my dead baby because of the previous miracle." Supresa said, "That day I was strengthened because I recalled that Jesus had raised a baby previously. I started calling out to Jesus Christ. . . . And again, the baby was raised from the dead in the name of Jesus. After that day, my house became like a hospital, with many people bringing sick family members to my house. Many people come to my house; some even stay for two weeks, but then they leave healed. God is doing miracles."[10]

. . .

As you can see from the stories in this chapter, resurrections still happen today. And I believe that the command to raise the dead is also for today. It wasn't just for Peter, Andrew, or James. It was for God's people—then and now. I hope these stories will encourage you and show you that God can work through you *today*, just as He did through His disciples. It will take the demonstration of the power of God to change the world in these last days.

. . .

By now we have firmly established that miracles—including the raising of the dead, as seen in this chapter—not only occurred in Bible times and in subsequent church history, but continue today.

As we move into the second part of the book, we will address and explain the reasons why many people in the West have difficulty believing in miracles. Then we will challenge their misguided and circular reasoning and, ultimately, show you God's truth regarding healing and how *you* can be used by God to bring healing to a hurting world.

PART TWO

THE PROBLEM WITH MIRACLES IN THE WESTERN MIND-SET

*And without faith it is impossible to please God, because
anyone who comes to him must believe that he exists
and that he rewards those who earnestly seek him.*

—HEBREWS 11:6

CHAPTER 6

RELIGION AND THE AGE OF ENLIGHTENMENT

The problem with miracles for the West is a recent development, beginning in the sixteenth century, but gaining much momentum in the eighteenth century. There was a time in the West when almost everyone believed in miracles. Even as the pendulum began to swing against such belief, there remained many scientists who believed in God, who was the source for the origin of creation, and who sustained the universe by His will. Only in the last three hundred years of Western civilization has there been the development of a worldview against supernatural thought among the intelligentsia. This section will detail the chain of events that led to that development.

However, any picture of a wholesale lack of belief in the supernatural today is quite misleading. Skepticism toward miracles is not nearly as strong among the Western populace as was once thought. Recent surveys reveal that, especially in the United States, a large majority of the population continue to believe in the supernatural.

A recent Harris poll revealed that 84 percent of the public believe that miracles occur today. A different poll phrased somewhat differently indicated that 73 percent of adults believed in miracles. Another poll revealed that 74 percent of eleven hundred physicians believed that miracles occur today, with 55 percent of them indicating they had seen medical miracles in their practices. Eighty-two percent of an Israeli survey indicated they believed in miracles, and 41 percent claimed to have experienced miracles in their own lives.[1] These statistics indicate that the influence of the "modern man" who cannot believe in miracles was greatly exaggerated by the intelligentsia of the eighteenth to twentieth centuries.

Jeremiah seems to represent the view of more people, even highly educated doctors, than of our universities. Jeremiah said to the Lord God, "You performed signs and wonders in Egypt and have continued them to this day, in Israel and among all mankind, and have gained the renown that is still yours" (Jer. 32:20). The tremendous influence of the Pentecostal and charismatic movements within Protestantism and Catholicism has created within the last hundred years a much greater openness to and belief in the miraculous. But it had not been this way, especially from the eighteenth and nineteenth centuries.

Let us now study the time line and the major influences that contributed to an intellectual dogma of unbelief by the majority of Westerners in the eighteenth to twentieth centuries and that held sway in the universities until the beginning of the twenty-first century. This dogma, which was not to be questioned and which caused a "dark age" to fall upon the thinking of many leaders in the church, has begun to be thrown off by many church leaders, as they come into a Rennaisance of their own in regard to understanding the "ways" of God in the realm of the supernatural.

The skepticism that developed during the 1700s in what is called the Age of Enlightenment resulted from several streams of thought that had gone through significant change during the prior two hundred years. Changes in religion, science, philosophy, politics, and theology all combined to dominate the world of ideas, including those concerning the reality of miracles.

Before the start of the Protestant Reformation in 1517, the reality of miracles had never been seriously challenged by the Catholic Church. Traditionally, Catholics had always believed in miracles. Even during the sixteenth century, healings were attributed to Luther and other Reformers.[2] But gradually, in response to perceived excesses, a tendency toward skepticism of the miraculous began to creep its way into the Reformation.

Martin Luther (1483–1546), the catalyst for the Protestant Reformation, had taught the *priesthood of all believers* and the *freedom of conscience* of the believers. Luther, however, was shaken by the impact of his own teachings on the left wing of the Reformation. Some adherents of the Anabaptists went too far, overemphasizing the Holy Spirit and putting more emphasis on the leading of the internal witness of the Holy Spirit than on the Bible. This in turn led to an excess in the prophetic ministry.

Additionally, this prophetic movement was part of the reason Thomas Munster, and others, taught that God wanted the people to revolt against the aristocracy, the land lords, and the establishment of the day, not just for religious or spiritual reasons but for economic reasons as well. So, they did, in what became known as the Peasants' Revolt. One hundred thousand peasants died in 1524 and 1525 during this rebellion.

The Reformation had produced the Lutherans in Germany; the Calvinists in France, named after John Calvin, a key leader in the Reformed faith; and Zwingli, another Reformed leader, in Switzerland. The Roman Catholics persecuted the Protestants because they believed the Protestants had departed from the faith and were heretics. Likewise, the Lutherans and Calvinist/Reformed believed the Anabaptists and other smaller groups of the Reformation, who had taken the principles of Luther and Calvin further, were also heretics. I have stood by the river in Switzerland where the Reformed, influenced by Zwingli, drowned the Anabaptists as heretics. This was not a time to question the doctrines of either the Catholic Church or the Protestant denominations.

The Calvinists' belief in the sovereignty of God led them to believe that all that happened, happened according to the will of God. This belief came perilously close to fatalism. Even our modern insurance companies' language reflects the lingering influence of this theology in calling tragedies, such as floods, tornadoes, earthquakes, and hurricanes, acts of God.

One of the greatest influences toward freedom of thought and the right to be skeptical was the loss of life due to the religious wars that broke out. From 1552 to 1598, between two million and four million people died during several religious wars that were fought in France between the Protestants and the Catholics. Between 1618 and 1648, again religious wars broke out between Catholics and Protestants. During this war, called the Thirty Years' War, eight hundred thousand people perished in Europe. In some areas so many men had died that they were heavily outnumbered by the women. This war was fought primarily in Germany, and so many men were killed in some parts of Germany that a special dispensation was given for men to have more than one wife to repopulate the areas. Religious dogmatism was seen to be partly to blame for the wars. There had also been religious wars in England and Denmark, as well as other Scandinavian countries.

The Catholic Church had always pointed to the miracles that were occurring within the church as vindication of its doctrine. But Luther's overreaction to the Peasants' Revolt and the anarchy it seemed to create with its emphasis upon subjective impressions, believed to be prophetic words from God, caused a rationalism to ultimately develop in Lutheranism. In time Lutheranism and Calvinism developed their own forms of scholastic dogmatism, with little emphasis upon subjective feelings, and a strong emphasis upon reason. This fear of present-day revelation that some Protestant sects embraced, along with the Catholic Church's insistence that miracles proved their doctrine was correct, resulted in the Protestants developing a belief that some of the gifts of the Holy Spirit (tongues, interpretation of tongues, prophecy, gifts of healing, and working of miracles) had ended with either the deaths of the apostles or the canonization of the Bible. This belief, known as *cessationism*, is still quite strong in America, which is the last stronghold of cessationism. The majority of Protestants then, who were becoming so influenced by rationalism, a major emphasis of the Enlightenment, considered the Catholics' belief in miracles to be superstitious.

In this historical context, when Europe, especially France, Germany, England, Denmark, and other Scandinavian countries, were sick of religious wars and the loss of lives and capital, the time was ripe for a reaction to Christian dogmatism. People began to question the teachings of the church, both Catholic and Protestant.

In this bloodied soil, voices would soon be heard that would value questioning not only religious beliefs, but all things. The Age of Reason, also known as the "Enlightenment," was about to be born. In time rationalism/skepticism would develop its own dogmatism, and science would become shackled to this new skepticism, with a dogmatism of its own. The only thing you could not question was the skeptical way of thinking and what resulted in a rejection of all things supernatural. The new dogmatism of naturalism and materialism would become as rigid as the old dogmatism of the church.

Rough dates for the Enlightenment are from 1650 to 1790.[3] The Enlightenment would bring a drastic change in perspective, especially in people's thinking about what is possible, basically ruling out the supernatural in the minds of many scientists and philosophers.

Eventually, this would even affect theologians.

CHAPTER 7

SCIENCE AND THE LAWS OF NATURE

In the 1700s, and especially the 1800s, the belief in God and what today we call "intelligent design" were replaced by a naturalistic view of the world. This happened first in the 1700s, in an intellectual movement called *deism*, the belief that though there is a God, who created everything, He doesn't intervene in the affairs of the world. Thomas Jefferson was a deist. Then, in the 1800s, a full-blown atheism among philosophers and many scientists began to develop. The new philosophy would be materialism, the belief that nothing exists except matter; and the philosophical view of naturalism, everything that happens can be explained in naturalistic terms without injecting the supernatural as an explanation. How did this happen?

Voltaire (1694–1778), a Frenchman, is seen as one of the most important persons in shifting the culture from believing without questioning to questioning everything and believing in nothing supernatural. He might be called the Father of the Enlightenment. His use of a pen name instead of his real name may be understood because he was so controversial. He not only attacked the church and its miracles; he attacked the very structure of society of his day. In his writings he referred to the church as the "infamy." In an essay that supposedly attacks those who renounce the divinity of Christ,

Voltaire suggested a "history" of how Jesus came to be considered divine by the church, supposedly over a period of centuries. Many of the ideas in the following passage originated before Voltaire, but few people expressed them as well.

> Christians spent three whole centuries in constructing little by little the apotheosis [raising to the status of a god] of Jesus. . . . At first . . . Jesus was regarded merely as a man inspired by God, then as a creature more perfect than the others. Sometime after he was given a place above the angels, as says Saint Paul. Every day added to his stature. He became an emanation of God manifested in time. That was not enough: he was held to be born before time itself. Finally he was made God, consubstantial with God.[1]

Voltaire's chronology ignores the fact that virtually all first- and second-century Christian writings and creeds universally accepted the divinity of Jesus. The great church councils of later centuries were not convened, as some insist, to establish Jesus' divinity, but largely to refute an upstart third-century movement to discredit it.

Voltaire was not a Christian. He was a materialist and a naturalist. He was a critic of society and a stronger critic of religion. In regard to the Bible he said, "In one hundred years this book will be forgotten." Instead of religion, he strongly supported Newtonian physics.

Sir Isaac Newton's physics was a new perspective on the world. Newton helped establish that there were laws that governed nature. The industrial revolution was also taking place, and it was the time of the machine. With this context it became a way of looking at the world: that it was a machine, our bodies functioned like a machine, and the laws of nature, more than the hand of God, were controlling or causing whatever happened. Newtonian physics would hold the day. Only with the discovery of quantum mechanics was the rigidity of Newtonian physics questioned.

One can still see the effect of Newton and the Enlightenment today. An example can be found in Dr. Herbert Benson's book on healing and faith. In *Timeless Healing: The Power and Biology of Belief,* Benson, a professor at Harvard Medical School, stated that he believes God hardwired our bodies to respond to faith. He was speaking there of a naturalistic cause and effect, for Benson does not believe faith can do anything that would break the laws of Newtonian physics. With this statement Benson reveals his unbelief in the supernatural in-breaking of God into our world. It also reveals the lasting effects of Enlightenment thinking upon science and upon theology. Benson also teaches at a seminary.

Another major influence on a culture that was becoming increasingly secular was William Paley (1743–1805). Paley was an English clergyman, apologist, and utilitarian. Utilitarians believe that the purpose of morality is to make life better by increasing the number of good things (such as pleasure and happiness) in the world and decreasing the number of bad things (such as pain and unhappiness). They reject moral codes or systems that consist of commands or taboos based on customs, traditions, or orders given by leaders or supernatural beings. Instead, utilitarians think that what makes a morality true or justifiable is its positive contribution to human (and perhaps nonhuman) beings. Utilitarian beliefs would have an effect on ethics during this time, removing the absolutes of a lawgiver and replacing these laws with a hedonistic, humanistic perspective (whatever makes a human happy or gives him or her pleasure is good).

Charles Darwin (1809–1882) added fuel to the humanistic fire when he developed the theory of evolution. His book *On the Origin of Species by Natural Selection* was written in 1859, and *The Descent of Man* in 1871. Darwin was an English natural historian and a geologist. He was not a Christian. There was a myth that he was a Christian, but this was because his earliest version of *The Origin of the Species* had been edited by his Christian wife, who edited out all his anti-God wording and his negative statements about Christianity. Later these were added back into his writings by someone else. As a naturalist Darwin did not allow for supernatural answers to questions.

Having already committed to naturalism, the view that nature itself, directed by its laws, is the cause of all things, rather than a supernatural being, God, it was easy for Darwin to develop his theory of evolution. He believed that all life has a common origin, from the inanimate to the animate and from lower life forms to higher life forms. This, he wrote, was the result of natural selection, or the survival of the fittest. "Fittest" didn't mean the strongest, he taught, but simply the most adapted to the environment.

This theory, in my opinion, requires a *science of the gaps*. What I mean is there is little evidence to prove the big jumps from one species to another. Science accuses religious people of believing in the *God of the gaps*. But the theory of evolution is wrought with unprovable assumptions without hard evidence, yet it is believed that with enough time, evolution can even bring about change from one species to another.

The theory of evolution was conceived to remove God from the world. You may be asking yourself, "Why would someone want to remove God from the picture?" In the historical context, some of the key leaders of the Enlightenment were hedonistic, desiring to have a sexuality without morality. Voltaire, for example, had a mistress who was married to someone else, making Voltaire a public adulterer. There was a desire to throw off moral restraint and to unshackle oneself from the restraints of the moral codes of religions, especially Christianity, because that was the predominant religion of Europe.

SCIENTISTS WITH A FAITH-BASED WORLDVIEW

In time, the theory of evolution would replace the belief in intelligent design, which pointed to a creator. However, it would be a mistake to think that all important scientists had an atheistic, antisupernatural perspective. Some of the greatest scientists have been theists, believing God could, and did, intervene in the world He had created. If we consider the period from the 1600s through the 1900s, we discover a number of significant contributors to modern scientific thought who also maintained a faith-based worldview.[2]

Sir Francis Bacon (1561–1627)

Bacon, one of whose stated goals was service to the church, was a philosopher known best for establishing the scientific method of inquiry based on experimentation and inductive reasoning. Although his work was based on such experimentation and reasoning, he rejected atheism. "It is true, that a little philosophy inclineth man's mind to atheism," he wrote, "but depth in philosophy bringeth men's minds about to religion; for while the mind of man looketh upon second causes scattered, it may sometimes rest in them, and go no further; but when it beholdeth the chain of them confederate, and linked together, it must needs fly to Providence and Deity."[3]

Johannes Kepler (1571–1630)

Kepler was a brilliant astronomer and mathematician and also a devout Lutheran. He studied light and developed the laws of planetary movement around the sun. He introduced the idea of force, moving astronomy powerfully in the direction of modern science. Kepler came close to discovering gravity before Newton did. Interestingly, his writings on astronomy contain statements hinting that space and the heavenly bodies represent the Trinity.[4] Contrary to the negative view of the Catholic Church against the sun-centered universe, Kepler was not persecuted for his open teaching of the sun-centered system. He was allowed as a Lutheran to stay in Catholic Graz as a professor (1595–1600)!

Galileo Galilei (1564–1642)

Galileo is remembered for, among other things, his conflict with the Roman Catholic Church. His controversial work on the solar system was published in 1633 and contained no proofs of a sun-centered system (Galileo's telescope discoveries did not indicate a moving earth). His one "proof," based on the tides, was invalid and ignored the correct, elliptical orbits of planets published twenty-five years earlier by Kepler. Since his work finished by putting the pope's favorite argument in the mouth of the simpleton in the dialogue, the pope, an old friend of Galileo's, was very offended. After his "trial" he was forbidden to teach the sun-centered system. That is when Galileo did his most useful theoretical work, which was on dynamics. He expressly said that the Bible cannot err, and saw his own system as an alternate interpretation of the biblical texts.

René Descartes (1596–1650)

Descartes was a French mathematician, scientist, and philosopher and has been called the father of modern philosophy. His school studies had made him dissatisfied with previous philosophy, so he developed a deep religious faith as a Roman Catholic. At age twenty-four he had a dream and felt the vocational call to bring knowledge together in one system of thought. His system began by asking what could be known if all else were doubted, suggesting the famous "I think; therefore, I am." What he really wanted was for his philosophy to be adopted as standard Roman Catholic teaching.

Descartes and Bacon are generally regarded as the key figures in the development of the scientific methodology. Both had systems in which God was important, and both seemed more devout than the average for their era.

Blaise Pascal (1623–1662)

Pascal was a French mathematician, physicist, inventor, writer, and theologian.[5] In mathematics, he published a treatise on the subject of projective geometry and established the foundation for probability theory. Pascal invented a mechanical calculator, and established the principles of vacuums and the pressure of air. He was raised a Roman Catholic, but in 1654 had a religious vision of God, which turned the direction of his study from science to theology. Pascal began publishing a theological work, *Lettres Provinciales*, in 1656. His most influential theological work, the *Pensées* ("Thoughts"), was a defense of Christianity, published after his death. The most famous concept from *Pensées* was Pascal's wager.[6] Pascal's last words were, "May God never abandon me."

Isaac Newton (1642–1727)

Isaac Newton was a figure of undisputed genius and innovation. In all his science (including chemistry), he saw mathematics and numbers as central. What is less well known is that he was devoutly religious and saw numbers as involved in understanding God's plan for history from the Bible. He did a considerable work on biblical numerology, and though aspects of his beliefs were not orthodox, he thought theology was very important. In his system of physics, God was essential to the nature and absoluteness of space. In the *Principia* he stated, "The most beautiful system of the sun, planets, and comets, could only proceed from the counsel and dominion of an intelligent and powerful Being."

Robert Boyle (1791–1867)

One of the founders and key early members of the Royal Society, Boyle gave his name to "Boyle's law" for gases, and also wrote an important work on chemistry. *Encyclopedia Britannica* says of him:

By his will he endowed a series of Boyle lectures, or sermons, which still continue, "for proving the Christian religion against notorious infidels . . ." As a devout Protestant, Boyle took a special interest in promoting the Christian religion abroad, giving money to translate and publish the New Testament into Irish and Turkish. In 1690 he developed his theological views in *The Christian Virtuoso*, which he wrote to show that the study of nature was a central religious duty.

Boyle wrote against atheists in his day (the notion that atheism is a modern invention is a myth), and was clearly much more devoutly Christian than the average writers of his era.

Michael Faraday (1791–1867)

Son of a blacksmith, Michael Faraday became one of the greatest scientists of the nineteenth century. His work on electricity and magnetism not only revolutionized physics, but led to many of the technologies we depend on today (including computers and telephone lines and, so, websites). Faraday was a devoutly Christian member of the Sandemanians, who significantly influenced him and strongly affected the way he approached and interpreted nature.

Gregor Mendel (1822–1884)

Mendel was the first to lay the mathematical foundations of genetics, in what came to be called "Mendelianism." Mendel was elected abbot of his monastery in 1868. His work remained comparatively unknown until the turn of the century, when a new generation of botanists began finding similar results and "rediscovered" him (though their ideas were not identical to his). Curiously, the 1860s were notable for formation of the X Club, which was dedicated to lessening religious influences and propagating an image of "conflict" between science and religion. One sympathizer was Darwin's cousin Francis Galton, whose scientific interest was in genetics (a proponent of eugenics-selective breeding among humans to "improve" the stock). He was writing how the "priestly mind" was not conducive to science while, at around the same time, an Austrian monk was making breakthroughs in genetics. The rediscovery of Mendel's work came too late to affect Galton's contribution.

William Thomson Kelvin (1824–1907)

Kelvin was foremost among the small group of British scientists who helped lay the foundations of modern physics. He was a very committed Christian, certainly more religious than the average scientist in his era. Interestingly, his fellow physicists George Gabriel Stokes (1819–1903) and James Clerk Maxwell (1831–1879) were also men of deep Christian commitment, in an era when many were nominal, apathetic, or anti-Christian. Lord Kelvin was an Old Earth creationist.

Max Planck (1858–1947)

Planck made many contributions to physics, but is best known for quantum theory, which revolutionized our understanding of the atomic and subatomic worlds. In his 1937 lecture "Religion and Naturwissenschaft," Planck contended that God is everywhere present, and that "the holiness of the unintelligible Godhead is conveyed by the holiness of symbols." Planck was a churchwarden from 1920 until his death, and believed in an almighty, all-knowing, beneficent God, though not necessarily a personal one.

Albert Einstein (1879–1955)

Einstein is probably the best-known and most highly revered scientist of the twentieth century, and is associated with major revolutions in our thinking about time, gravity, and the conversion of matter to energy ($E=mc^2$). Although he never came to belief in a personal God, he recognized the impossibility of a non-created universe.

CONTEMPORARY SCIENTISTS WHO BELIEVE IN INTELLIGENT DESIGN

Today, there are several scientists and philosophers who look at the complexity of design and once again believe in intelligent design, including the following:

> **Michael Behe,** who has developed the argument for design from biochemistry and has published more than thirty-five articles in refereed biochemical journals
>
> **Ralph Seelke,** a microbiologist at the University of Wisconsin–Superior, who has researched Dr. Behe's ideas in the laboratory, using mutant bacteria
>
> **Scott Minnich,** a microbiologist at the University of Idaho, who credits the design paradigm to leading to new insights in his lab research
>
> **Wolf-Ekkehard Lönnig,** a German geneticist who suggests that intelligent design provides fruitful hints for giraffe research[7]
>
> **Professor Richard Smalley** (1943–2005), winner of the 1996 Nobel Prize in chemistry, who has stated publicly that based on strictly scientific grounds, he is persuaded that evolution is impossible and believes the burden of proof is on those who doubt the Genesis narrative

Guillermo Gonzalez, astronomer, who has opened a new frontier
for the intelligent design paradigm with his arguments from
cosmology

Sir Fred Hoyle (1915–2001), an English astronomer and mathematician, who contended that any scientist who had studied the origin
of life with an unbiased mind must conclude that "biomaterials
with their amazing measure or order must be the outcome of
intelligent design. No other possibility I have been able to think of."[8]

Some have tried to resolve the issue of evolution by the theory called
theistic evolution. One such person was Teilhard de Chardin, a French
idealist philosopher and Jesuit priest who trained as a paleontologist and
geologist and took part in the discovery of Peking man. The problem
with this solution is that Darwin's theory of evolution was directed
by natural selection, which in no way is directed by God. Theistic
evolution makes God rather than natural selection the designer who has
purpose. This is not the primary scientific understanding of evolution.

I find it easier, when I consider the complexity of the universe and
of the human cell, to believe in an intelligent designer, a lawgiver for
the natural laws, and one who can use higher laws—not yet known to
science—to work in His creation. This understanding makes miracles
not violations of natural law, but the utilization of higher laws. For
example, the law of aerodynamics displaces the law of gravity, allowing
metal to fly. It takes less faith on my part to believe in God as an
intelligent designer who has created not only laws to govern nature,
but moral laws to govern society and family life. I believe the Creator
has left an operator's manual to help us understand how we are to live
in such a way as not to be self-destructive or to undermine society.

In the next chapter we will turn our attention from science to
philosophy, considering its impact on the Enlightenment and the
Enlightenment's resulting skepticism.

CHAPTER 8

PHILOSOPHY AND THEOLOGY

Not only were naturalist scientists trying to throw off the restraints of Christianity during the Age of Enlightenment; so were philosophers. We have already considered Voltaire, who was not so much a philosopher as a critical satirist of Christianity and the social institutions. Two other philosophers of note are David Hume and Ludwig Fuerbach.

David Hume (1711–1776) is regarded as one of the most influential philosophers of the Western world. His influence contributed to the rational theology of German theologians in the Age of Enlightenment, a theology based on a philosophical presupposition that miracles have not happened and do not happen. Hume's argument against miracles, however, is circular. It is based on the assumption that miracles have not occurred and do not occur.

Hume's understanding of and definition for miracles is a departure from the biblical understanding of miracles, and by his definition they are impossible—again, based on circular reasoning. He would argue that even if there was credible evidence of a miracle occurring, one should not believe it, and should never trust the report of a person who claimed to have seen or experienced a miracle. Hume also had a secular understanding of nature that removed God.

Hume noted that there were not many testimonies of miracles occurring. In his time this was greatly truer than it is today. In the twenty-first century, unlike the eighteenth century, there are hundreds of thousands of miraculous claims. Hume also noted in his day that the claims were from the uneducated rather than the educated. Today many scholars with PhDs, MDs, and other master's and doctorate degrees claim they have witnessed miracles. Hume believed everything that happened could be explained in a naturalistic way without reference to God. Hume was definitely not a Christian; neither was he a theist. At best he was a mild deist, but many believe he was an atheist.

Hume's philosophical system was not popular when he first wrote, and was quite rejected at the time by the academia of Great Britain. Only later did his views become popular. In time his views would be very influential upon the Enlightenment. They would influence historiography by causing the writers of history not to accept as true anything that appeared to violate the known laws of nature. These stories, tales, legends, or myths, as they were referred to, could not have happened simply because they could not happen based on Hume's understanding of reality. German theology would later reflect this view as well. All things supernatural would be seen as having no basis in reality; they could not happen; they should not be accepted as true, according to Hume. This resulted in liberal theology that rejected all accounts of miracles, even those the Bible attributed to Jesus. In time, almost all theological schools and Christian colleges in Europe and in America held to this view or a form of this view.

It is sad that the cessationist view of Protestantism of Hume's day made his argument stronger, for there were almost no miraculous claims in Protestantism in his time. His argument would have been much less persuasive if Pentecostalism and the charismatic form of

Christianity, which has so many healings and miracles, had existed in Hume's day. Dr. Craig Keener, one of the leading English-speaking Bible commentators of the twenty-first century, points this out in his two-volume work *Miracles*.[1]

Ludwig Feuerbach (1804–1872), a proponent of atheism, liberalism, and materialism, was a German who studied under Hegel. Feuerbach's philosophy can be summed up by the dictum "the rational alone is real," meaning that all reality is capable of being expressed in rational categories. His goal was to reduce reality to a more synthetic unity within the system of absolute idealism.

In 1941 Feuerback published *The Essence of Christianity*, which influenced later German theologians as well as politicians. He believed that Western culture and its institutions, including Christianity, would be superseded, and that Christianity itself had long passed from reason and from the actual life of mankind, remaining nothing more than a fixed idea. God, he taught, was nothing more than the self-projection of our human making. Instead of God making us, we made God. To Feuerbach, God was more of an impersonal force, a law, a quality, like love. To believe that God had a separate existence from humankind was a false belief or religion. Feuerbach thus did not believe in divine revelation, and he alleged that the Lord's Supper was a materialistic superstition and contributed to immorality. His philosophy would attempt to explain spiritual phenomena from a purely naturalistic perspective.

Feuerbach's materialistic atheism had a strong influence on Karl Marx and Friedrich Engels, the founders of communism. His influence on these men alone would have terrible consequences for Europe. They, like Feuerbach, would deny anything that wasn't material. In 1868 Feuerbach read Marx's *Das Kapital* and joined the Social Democratic Party, one of the first Marxist-influenced parties in the world.

THE IMPACT OF THE ENLIGHTENMENT
UPON THEOLOGY[2]

It is important to remember that during the Enlightenment, the basis of religious authority experienced a dramatic shift. Religious authority moved from the Protestant basis of biblical authority to the human authority of perception and reason. The Enlightenment era is generally regarded as the watershed in thought about miracles.[3] During this time when there was a desire to verify by empirical evidence, there was a great debate between Christian apologists who were themselves scientists and the new skepticism of the Enlightenment. Jon Ruthven points out that these were famous scientists who believed that the miracles themselves proved the existence of God.

Such scientists as "Bishop John Wilkins, founder of the Royal Society for the Advancement of Science, Sir Robert Boyle, 'the father of chemistry . . . ,' Sir Isaac Newton, and Archbishop Tillotson were theists and today we would call them proponents of intelligent design."[4] Newton believed the laws of nature were laws established by God. Each of these men believed that nature pointed to a Creator, and they further believed that miracles in the Bible, as well as contemporary healings and miracles, proved the existence of God, though it must be said there were not nearly as many healings and miracles taking place at this time as there have been for the last one hundred years, and especially the last sixty years.

The new apologists of the 1700s and 1800s believed that reason would be able to come to faith in Christ when the miracles and the prophetic fulfillments were made known. This belief was supported by a philosophy that came out of Scotland, known as Scottish Common Sense Realism.[5] A modern-day writer who follows this line of thinking is Josh McDowell. His *Evidence that Demands a Verdict* and *More Evidence that Demands a Verdict* are based on common-sense philosophy, as it was called in the eighteenth century.

Against this new rational approach to faith based on miracles rose the deists, who not only didn't believe in divine revelation; they tried to dispute the miracles that were supportive of the argument of divine revelation. Philosophy became anti-supernatural and anti-Christian to a great degree.

Hume's arguments, mentioned earlier, were not as influential in his time as they would be later. They were rehashed ideas already presented before Hume. Much more important during this time than Hume was Conyers Middleton, from whom Hume drew.

The Influence of Conyers Middleton

Conyers Middleton (1683–1750) was a deist. He wrote, *A Free Inquiry into the Miraculous Powers which are supposed to have subsisted in the Christian church from the earliest ages through several successive centuries. By which it is shown that we have no sufficient reason to believe, upon the authority of the primitive fathers, that any such powers were continued to the church after the days of the Apostles.* (In his time titles explained the book and were long.) Conyers had six major reasons for not believing in miracles past the age of the apostles:

1. That they [miracles] were all of such a nature, and performed in such a manner, as would necessarily inject a suspicion of fraud and delusion.

2. That the cures and beneficial effects of them were either false, or imaginary, or accidental.

3. That they tend to confirm the idlest of all errors and superstitions.

4. That the integrity of the witnesses is either highly questionable, or their credulity at least so gross, as to render them unworthy of any credit.

5. That they were not only vain and unnecessary, but generally speaking, so trifling also, as to excite nothing but contempt.

6. That the belief and defense of them are the only means in the world that can possibly support, or that does in fact give any sort of countenance, to the modern impostures in the Romish Church.[6]

Middleton's attack on the miracles of the Roman Catholic Church, John Wesley recognized as an attack on Christianity. Middleton, like the twentieth-century B. B. Warfield, would heavily use the character assignation tactic that state's attorneys use against defense witnesses, and vice versa. The preceding six points were full of efforts to discredit the trustworthiness of the historical witnesses to healing, signs and wonders, and miracles occurring in the history of the church.

Middleton would also use the historical-critical arguments of the newly developed German theologians that denied as possible anything that was supernatural. This view of history was based on the presupposition that miracles were impossible; they therefore had to be explained away. This at first was done by offering a naturalistic, non-supernatural explanation, later by giving the accounts a legendary or mythical interpretation.

B. B. Warfield's Influence

In the twentieth century B. B. Warfield (1851–1921) wrote *Counterfeit Miracles*. I was told in my college religious studies courses that "Warfield's *Counterfeit Miracles* was the last nail in the coffin of belief in the continuation of miracles." Warfield, like his predecessors, attacked the witnesses who claimed miracles had happened or were happening. He also used the arguments that the liberal theologians used to discredit the miracles in the Bible, for discrediting the miracles of the post-apostolic age. Warfield accepted the historicity of the biblical miracles, however, rejecting the very arguments he used for discrediting the post-apostolic miracles. Thus, his historical method was internally inconsistent, thereby invalidating one-half of his argument against miracles continuing past the canonization of the Bible. The ground would be laid for further attacks on the supernatural dimension of Christian faith.

HERE COME THE LIBERALS

Ernst Troeltsch (1865–1923)

Troeltsch wrote *The Historical Challenge to Miracles*. Troeltsch's objection to miracles: the principle of historical analogy. In essence this principle states the historian has no right to accept as historical fact the account of a past event for which he has no analogy in the present.

Consider this example: If one were to read of a great battle in ancient times in which one army massacres another without suffering a single casualty itself, one would be suspect of its authenticity.

So the argument against miracles goes, "God never does miracles today; at least I've never seen one. Therefore, I have no reason to believe that He did them in the past." Today, this argument from analogy would actually prove miracles rather than discredit them. Pentecostal, charismatic, and Third-Wave Christians have reversed the context regarding analogy from the eighteenth and nineteenth centuries, when there were so few miracles in comparison to the twenty-first century. The lack of miracles in the preceding centuries was due to Protestantism reaping what it had sown. Its cessationist theology was the reason for their meager experience of the supernatural.

Rudolf Bultmann (1888–1976)

Troeltsch would be followed by Rudolf Bultmann, who wrote *Theology of the New Testament* volume 1 in 1951 and volume 2 in 1955. Bultmann believed that the modern thinker could not embrace the worldview of the New Testament or believe in the miracles. He said, "If you use a lightbulb you can't believe in miracles."

Paul Tillich (1886–1965)

Paul Tillich was another famous theologian who denied the miraculous aspect of Christianity. While I was going to college, I read his *Systematic Theology*. I was appalled that he stated that his faith would not be destroyed if it was discovered that Jesus wasn't really raised from the dead. Reading Tillich destroyed the faith of one of my best friends and fellow students in religious studies in college. He left the ministry having lost his faith specifically from his studies. It also was detrimental to my faith. It would take years for this type of teaching to be overcome in my life. What helped the most was seeing God deliver people from demons and heal their bodies. Later I would witness not just healings, but miracles, and even meet people raised from the dead, as mentioned in an earlier chapter.

Van A. Harvey (1926–)

Van Harvey wrote *The Historian and the Believer*. This was the book I had to read in the last year of my master of divinity program at a Baptist seminary that opened my eyes to the presuppositions upon which almost all my college and master's level seminary work was based. I realized that the higher-critical method I had been taught to use in interpreting the Bible was based on an understanding of history that did not allow for the supernatural, an understanding that started with the assumption that miracles cannot occur nor have they ever occurred.

I determined that I did not believe this assumption, but I did believe—not just believed; I *knew*—healing and miracles took place, because I had been healed. I understood that this assumption did not allow for the future to be known prophetically, and therefore would reject prophecies by saying they were written during or after the events described as future were already taking place. I understood how this had affected the date setting of certain books in the Bible. I realized I had been taught a system of theology whose basic assumptions regarding what was possible and what wasn't were in stark disagreement with my own beliefs.

Harvey Cox (1929–)

Harvey Cox, another theologian influenced by liberalism, wrote *The Secular City* in 1965. The book's title was based on his observation that the mainline churches in the cities were greatly declining in attendance. These large, once-full church buildings were now attended by a diminishing handful of members. He concluded that cities were going to become secular because the churches could not reach the secular citizens there. Only the rural communities would remain faithful to the Christian faith. Dr. Cox likely believed with Bultmann that modern people would no longer have faith in Christianity, or at least not have faith in a supernatural understanding of Christianity.

In 1995, after several years of traveling the world, investigating Pentecostal and charismatic churches, Dr. Cox wrote *Fire from Heaven: The Rise of Pentecostal Spirituality and the Reshaping of Religion in the 21st Century*. This book was an acknowledgment that his first book, so hailed as prophetic by others, had in fact been wrong. He had underestimated the power of the storefront Pentecostal churches in the cities in the 1960s. The cities of the world, instead of becoming more secular, were becoming more open to the spiritual, especially the Pentecostal-charismatic form of Christianity.

This reminded me of Saint Augustine. He, too, when he was young in ministry, had made negative statements about healing and miracles in his day. When he was much older, however, in his famous book *City of God* was a section titled "Retractions." There he admitted to being knowledgeable of many miracles and healings that were occurring in his bishopric. Further, he was aware of other bishops who likewise were still seeing healings and miracles. Augustine would not be the first or last pastor or theologian to reverse his or her opinion regarding healing and miracles.

CHAPTER 9

EXPLAINING AWAY THE MIRACULOUS

When someone is in an impossible situation, when the prognosis is terrible, and there is no hope medically, and then there is a prayer and the person is healed, what do many in the medical field or naturalists usually call it? They certainly don't use the word *miracle*, or even *healing*. Their reasoning and worldview will not allow for such an explanation. Their philosophical dogmatism cannot accept the obvious. They instead call it something like "spontaneous remission" of the disease. Or it's an "anomaly." The explanation often is, "There must have been a misdiagnosis." Sometimes the answer is in blaming the medical equipment, which must have given a false reading. Sometimes the response is, "We can't explain it now, but one day we will be able to give a naturalistic explanation for why the person was so quickly healed. We don't understand the power of the mind." And, yes, the mighty placebo has been given a lot of glory. Even when the conditions that are necessary and conducive for the placebo effect to work are missing, the placebo of the gaps gets the glory.

And the fact that the person's health seems to have turned for the better right after or during the prayer, well, "that was just a coincidence." I am amazed by how many "coincidences" I have seen, and have heard of from others.

The one thing that really irritates me is when you have a healing that is definitely related to a prayer, you tell the doctor your testimony, you explain how you hadn't been able to be restored to health through all the best efforts of the medical field, and then either immediately or within a few hours of the prayer, you were healed—and the doctor doesn't write it in your medical notes. This was the case twice in my life, but nothing was put in the notes, even when I was explicit about the connection to prayer due to the timing of the prayer and the timing of the healing.

In this chapter we will consider how miracles have been and are interpreted by those who have a philosophical worldview, an understanding of reality, that allows for miracles. These conservative theologians are divided into two camps: the continuationist and the cessationist. We shall consider the biblical basis for both positions.

THE BIBLICAL DEFINITION AND THE
ARGUMENTS OF CONSERVATIVE CHRISTIANS

The biblical definition of a miracle is quite different from the scientific one. Our modern understanding of a miracle is that it can't have happened through any natural means. It must be instant, and it must be 100 percent. If there has been any other treatment that would rule out the definition of miracle, then it could not have been a miracle, because there could be a delayed healing from the treatment. The Bible sees the miraculous more from a perspective of timing. If the answer comes in relationship to prayer, even if there could be a natural explanation, then it is a miracle, because God is seen to work both in nature and above nature. The issue is the timing of the occurrence of the sign, wonder, healing, or miracle.

For example, during a terrible drought in south Texas, a board member of my ministry, Richard Holcomb, believed God told him there would be several inches of rain by a certain date that was a couple of months off. In Kerrville, Texas, in 2002, it had rained very little for four months (February–May) and it was a dry season.[1] On June 1, 2002, Richard heard God say to him, *"Pray for at least 17.2 inches of rain to fall in June and July."* There was no precedent for this amount of rain in those months, as historically they are very dry months in Texas. Richard obeyed, however, and the Texas Department of Agriculture reported that by August 1, 2002, 24.23 inches of rain had fallen between June 1 and July 31.

How do conservative Christians understand or explain what seems miraculous? Those who believe in the miraculous today say either God did it, one of God's angels did it, or God did it through one of His human servants. Those who do not believe in present-day miracles or miraculous gifts of the Holy Spirit explain that the Devil did it, or one of his angels did it, or the Devil or demon did it through a human servant. An example of this mind-set would be Simon the Sorcerer—the Great One of Samaria. Yet, when he saw the power of God working through Philip, he left the kingdom of darkness to become part of the kingdom of light.

I have witnessed two modern-day "Simons." Both were in Mozambique. One was the most renowned witch doctor in the city of Beira and surrounding area. The other was the most renowned witch doctor of northern Mozambique. He walked with poisonous puff adders hanging around his neck. Both gave their lives to Jesus when they encountered Dr. Heidi Baker. The first witch doctor's live-in lover was deaf. When they accepted Jesus, her deafness was healed when she was baptized.

Augustine had much to say about the baptism in the Holy Spirit, and the charisms of the Spirit. In relationship to water baptism, he stated, "We must not think that those who have received a valid baptism have also automatically [*continuo*] received the Holy Spirit."[2]

Augustine's quote, in context, is referring to the baptism in the Holy Spirit. When Christianity became the official religion of the empire, the standards for entry were lowered, and the degree of sincerity was lower for many of the so-called converts. With this change, the expectation for the charisms to be given, even manifested at baptism, became less and less.

At the time of the Reformation, the Catholic Church faced Luther with the charge that it still had miracles, which proved its doctrine was correct. Luther adopted cessationism as a defense against Catholicism, and as a basis of placing all authority only in the Bible, and he was forced to accredit the source of the miracles after the close of the canon to false miracles at best and demonic activity at worst. The only true miracles were the ones in the Bible; there were no miracles after the close of the canon.[3]

John Calvin's followers today are more cessationist than he was. He believed that if someone were to go to a region where there was no church, he could expect to see miracles and healings until the church was established. The miracles and healings would then cease in that region.

Dr. Robert Culpepper, a former professor of theology for the Southern Baptist foreign mission board, wrote that he had once been a cessationist. However, he had changed his position due to his experience and the realization that biblically speaking, he had been wrong.[4]

CHRISTIAN CESSATIONIST AND CHRISTIAN CONTINUATIONIST BELIEFS ABOUT MIRACLES

Cessationists (from the word *cease*) believe that the gifts of healing, miracles, prophecy, tongues, and interpretation of tongues ended with the canonization of the Bible or the death of the last apostles, or the disciples of the last disciples. One can see by the multiple options for when the aforementioned gifts were supposed to cease that there are varied opinions within the cessationist camp. Obviously, this group would not believe in the continuation of signs and wonders or miracles after the apostolic age. They don't reject the signs and wonders, healings, and miracles, however, on the basis of naturalism or materialism. No, instead the rejection is based on theological reasons.

The cessationist believes that miracles and healings are given to authenticate and vindicate true doctrine, and were performed by the apostles. The Bible was written mainly by apostles or those who personally knew one of the apostles. If signs and wonders, healings, and miracles happened through someone today, then that individual could claim to be an apostle and could therefore write scripture today. This would mean the Bible would not be closed and that new books to the Bible could be added. Since cessationists assert that the canon of Scripture is closed, it is, therefore, not possible for anyone to have gifts of healing today.

Continuationists, on the other hand, believe that the gifts of healing, miracles, prophecy, tongues, and interpretation of tongues have continued in the world and in the church. They also believe, however, that the Bible has been finished, and nothing will be added to it. Therefore, any healings and miracles we see are still today what the apostle John called them in his gospel: "signs."

These signs and wonders point to the coming of Jesus back to the earth to establish His rule over the earth. They are present because in Jesus' first coming, He inaugurated the kingdom of God. It is both present and future. It is here, but not in its complete form. Until then we live in the now and the not-yet. Not everyone is healed, and they won't be until the second coming of Jesus. But people are being healed, by the hundreds of thousands. Jesus said that anyone who believed in Him would do what He had done, and greater works than these would he or she do (John 14:12). Mark, author of the second gospel, wrote that signs and wonders followed the preaching of the gospel—indeed, God confirmed the gospel with signs and wonders (see Mark 16:20).

Both the cessationist and the continuationist are Christians who believe the Bible is a spiritual book that reveals how to be reconciled to God and what God's nature is like. They believe in the historicity of the Bible—that all the miracles Jesus did really happened and were not legendary embellishments or myths.

Liberal Christians believe the Bible reveals truths about God and how to be reconciled to God as well. They do not believe in miracles, however, even the ones in the Bible. They would give these miracles a naturalistic explanation or consider them little more than stories that reveal spiritual truths. Ironically, I have found it often easier for a liberal Christian to change his belief in God not giving His gifts today, including healings and miracles, than for a very fundamentalist, Bible-believing Christian to accept that signs and wonders, healings and miracles, and gifts of the Spirit happen today. The latter group explains the apparent healing or miracle as a lying sign and wonder worked by the Devil.

The group of Protestants that believe most strongly in present-day signs and wonders, healings, and miracles, are the Pentecostals and the charismatics. This group makes up the largest and the fastest-growing group of Christians in the world today. Where the Catholic Church is growing the fastest is also among the charismatic Catholics. Pope Francis is a charismatic, as is the new archbishop of the Anglican Church, Justin Welby. Archbishop Welby believes that the hope of re-evangelizing Europe is connected to power evangelism.[5] Power evangelism is dependent upon the power of God's Spirit to work today as it did in the time of Jesus and the first few centuries of the church.

In the appendices, you will find the many references to signs and wonders, healings, and miracles, as well as other terms used in the Bible that display the supernatural power of God. But next, we will look at the forces God used to restore to the church a much greater openness to the miraculous power of God, and to His healing and His miracles to occur in our modern era.

CHAPTER 10

RECOVERING THE MINISTRY OF HEALING

Johann Blumhardt (1805–1880) was a German Lutheran theologian and pastor. He had been trained in liberal theology at the University of Tübingen. Blumhardt was one of the first Protestants to experience healing. After a young woman and her brother were delivered from demons, a revival broke out the next day. When the demon came out the preceding night, it yelled, "Jesus is Victor!" This became the theme for Blumhardt. Healings soon broke out in his ministry as well. So many people were coming to Christ and so many being healed that the people flocked to his church from other parishes, and some from quite a distance. This caused jealousy and controversy within the Lutheran churches in the area. Finally, Blumhardt was told he had to stop praying for the sick. Instead, he resigned, moved to a spa-health center, and continued the ministry of healing.

When liberal theologian Rudolf Bultmann was questioned about the public healing ministry of Johann Blumhardt, Bultmann said it was a "legend" and an "abomination" to Protestantism. He did not try to examine the evidence, and he did not study the ministry of Blumhardt. He had already assumed healing was impossible, so he didn't bother to check out if his assumption was true.[1]

Blumhardt was not the only person who was beginning to rediscover healing in Europe in the nineteenth century. A florist, Dorothea Trudel in Switzerland, also experienced healing, especially for people with mental illness. She would become famous for the gift of healing associated with her. These two Europeans would be instrumental in the development of what became known in America as the *faith cure movement*.

A homeopathic doctor, Charles Cullis (1833–1892), would cross the Atlantic to visit both, returning to America to begin healing rooms. Andrew Murray (1828–1917), a famous Christian devotional writer, would visit a faith cure home in London, run by W. E. Broadman, where he would be healed of a throat problem that prohibited him from speaking from 1879 to 1881. Before his healing he had met with Otto Stockmayer, the disciple and successor to Dorothea Trudel. Though Murray had been trained as a Dutch Reformed cessationist, once he was healed he had to teach and write about healing.

A. B. Simpson (1843–1919), trained as a Presbyterian cessationist, would be healed of a heart condition that would cause him to have to resign from ministry. A. J. Gordon (1836–1895), trained as a Baptist, would also become a leader in the developing faith cure movement. He was a scholar-pastor who read his Greek New Testament every morning. His book *The Ministry of Healing* would become a classic. B. B. Warfield would write a whole chapter in *Counterfeit Miracles* dealing with Gordon's arguments. There were many others used to birth the faith cure movement, which became the most controversial topic in Christianity in America from 1875 to 1900.[2]

Note that this was a full twenty-five years before the birth of Pentecostalism. The ministry of healing was not a Pentecostal development, but Pentecostals were the first to emphasize the "gifts" of healing, not content to limit healing to the promises of God in the Scripture, which was the emphasis of the faith cure movement. Again in the twenty-first century, scholars who once were liberal, who previously denied miracles, have had their own experience of needing to now defend healing and miracles.

While I could name many theologians and pastors who also were used to restore faith in physical healing, space does not allow me the luxury. I will just mention two such scholars. Craig Keener (1960–), whom I mentioned earlier, is a Baptist scholar, now teaching in Asbury Seminary's doctoral program. He has written what I believe to be the best book on healing and miracles of the twenty-first century, in which he also explains the weakness of the argument of David Hume and his followers.[3]

Andrew Park was my mentor for the doctoral program at United Theological Seminary. At one time he was the most liberal theologian at the seminary. He is one of the most famous process theologians in the world. There was a transformation in Dr. Park, however, during the time he was the mentor for my doctoral group. Today, Dr. Park is a strong defender of healing and miracles. Other professors at the seminary have had a similar change of beliefs regarding healing and miracles. Dr. Park and the academic dean of the seminary, Dr. David Watson, have both had their own experiences of seeing someone healed when they prayed for them with the laying on of hands.

THE POWER OF GOD IN
SIGNS AND WONDERS

The ease with which we find evidence of God's power touching everyday lives in Scripture should fill us with hope since we know that Jesus is the same yesterday, today, and forever (Heb. 13:8). And nowhere do we see that more plainly than in the written documentary of early church life, the book of Acts. Jack Deere, in his book *Surprised by the Voice of God*, noted that in every chapter of Acts except chapter 17, we see an example of or a reference to supernatural revelatory communication from God to His servants.[4] And note that this activity did not occur just with those we think of as apostles, for we see powerful signs and wonders demonstrated through "ordinary" folks, like Philip, Stephen, Barnabas, Agabus, and most notably, Ananias, who is referred to merely as "a disciple" (Acts 9:10–19). This otherwise unknown man received messages from the Lord to find Saul and pray for him to restore his sight, and to lay hands on Saul that he might be filled with the Holy Spirit. His initial reluctance is understandable given Saul's murderous intents, but still he obeyed and opened the door for much more revelation to come through Paul's authorship of Scripture. In Acts 10, God communicated to an unsaved man, Cornelius, telling him how to find Peter, who would bring him a message by which he would be saved.

Signs and wonders are a normal occurrence in the kingdom of God, and they show up in a variety of New Testament texts. I want to encourage you to take the time to read the appendices to see for yourself how pregnant the Bible is with the supernatural power of God. May the realization of the continuation of the miraculous today cause you to hunger to know personally this supernatural God. May you be encouraged to strengthen your relationship with Him, desiring to not only speak to Him, but to believe He will speak to you. He speaks in many and various ways; through the Bible as the Spirit communicates to you through its stories and wisdom, theology, and doctrines; through prophecy and words of knowledge; through divine appointments, where God sets up a meeting with the right person to say the right thing at the right time; and through visions and dreams.

THE VERIFICATION OF HEALINGS AND MIRACLES

Candy Brown, PhD, religious studies professor at Indiana University–Bloomington, is becoming one of the most notable researchers on healing in America. She is the author of several books on healing, with one dedicated to a study of the attempt to verify healing from both the medical and the Christian clergy perspectives. Entitled *Testing Prayer: Science and Healing*, it describes her efforts with a team both in Brazil and in Mozambique to verify the healing of eyesight and deafness. Having received a grant from the Templeton Foundation for the research, she worked alongside a team of researchers that included a medical doctor, a PhD who had been involved in research at Washington University in St. Louis, and also a professor at Indiana University, and a renowned sociologist of religion. Their work, "Study of the Therapeutic Effects of Proximal Intercessory Prayer (STEPP) on Auditory and Visual Impairments in Rural Mozambique," was published in the peer-reviewed *Southern Medical Journal*.

A few years before Dr. Brown wrote *Testing Prayer*, her husband had gone on a trip to Brazil with me. There he saw several people healed when he prayed, including two brothers, both with blind eyes that were white instead of brown; and hundreds healed through the prayers of fellow team members. He asked if I would be interested in representing one of the speakers at a conference at St. Louis University, where his wife, Candy, a Harvard graduate, was a professor. The conference was titled "Healing: Catholic, Protestant, and Medical Perspectives," and was sponsored by both the medical school and the divinity school of the university. She would be a speaker, along with Dr. Francis MacNutt and his wife, Judith, well-known Catholics in the healing ministry; a psychiatrist, a theologian, a medical professor, and a hospital chaplain would be the other speakers. I would represent the Protestant minister on the panel.

This experience lit a fire in me regarding the need for better verification of healings related to prayer. A few years later I sponsored a symposium on healing at the Yale University chapel. I invited Dr. Candy Brown and her husband, Dr. Josh Brown, professors at the

University of Indiana–Bloomington; John Peteet, an associate professor of psychiatry at Harvard University Medical School; Dr. Harold Koenig, a psychiatrist and medical professor from Duke University, who was one of the prolific writers on the relationship between healing and spirituality in the United States; Dr. Stephen Mory, a psychiatrist who taught for Vanderbilt University; and Drs. Francis and Judith MacNutt, mentioned earlier.

On the way to take Dr. Koenig to the airport, I asked him about how to conduct verification studies of healing. He told me that a verified healing needs to be something that cannot be ascribed to spontaneous remission. It also needed to be something that could be tested in the place the meetings were occurring, without involving high-tech machines. He suggested testing vision with eye charts, and testing hearing loss with machines that could measure hearing levels.

This is precisely the experiment that Dr. Candy Brown did with her team funded by the Templeton Foundation. They tested for eyesight and hearing using the methods suggested by Dr. Koenig. The study was published in the *Southern Medical Journal*, volume 103, issue 9, in September 2010. As stated earlier, it was entitled "Study of the Therapeutic Effects of Proximal Intercessory Prayer (STEPP) on Auditory and Visual Impairments in Rural Mozambique," conducted by Dr. Candy Brown, Dr. Stephen Mory, Dr. Rebecca Williams, and Dr. Michael McClymond.

This study reviewed proximal intercessory prayer (PIP) as a type of alternative therapy and its effects on health. PIP describes close proximity prayer, usually with the laying on of hands. The team used an audiometer to evaluate hearing improvement and vision charts to evaluate eyesight improvement. Results indicate improvements in both hearing and vision after PIP prayer. The study's purpose was to verify whether or not sight and hearing problems improved following prayer. The team of researchers did rule out that the results were due to the placebo effect or to hypnosis by indicating in charts the probability of both upon the physical problems studied. Then they charted the percentage of those who did substantially improve, whose improvement was much higher than could have been statistically predicted based on the placebo effect and/or hypnosis—thus ruling out the results as due to either of these.

These studies were conducted on two of my international ministry trips in Mozambique and Brazil. Candy references Global Awakening, the Apostolic Network of Global Awakening (ANGA), and me a total of 352 times in *Testing Prayer: Science and Healing*. In the book she compiled and contributed to *Global Pentecostal and Charismatic Healing*, she wrote an entire chapter on the ministry of Global Awakening and its influence on the majority world and the Western world.[5]

CHAPTER 11

VERIFYING HEALING

I worked on my doctoral degree in ministry from 2011 to 2013. My thesis is titled "A Study of the Effects of Christian Prayer on Pain or Mobility Restrictions from Surgery Involving Implanted Materials" (SIM).[1] I chose this topic because I had been seeing people receive healing from chronic pain and mobility restrictions and wanted to do a more thorough investigation of these types of healing to try to verify healing was occurring in response to prayer. I had learned how the physical therapy field tested for improvement of conditions through examining the range of motion and self-reporting pain levels.

I not only wanted to determine whether or not people were being healed; I also wanted to determine through research if there were variables that would contribute to healing. My research determined that three variables proved important to healing: (1) a personal theology for healing, (2) training in the practical principles of healing, and (3) a previous experience with healing.[2] Three other variables I believed would contribute to greater probability of healing were: (1) the gift of the word of knowledge's impact upon a person to create much more expectation (faith) for healing, (2) commanding prayers rather than intercessory or petitionary prayers, and (3) the person's expectation of healing. The study reported on those who had an improvement of at least 80 percent, significantly higher than the benefit of a second surgery, which was 10–20 percent.

The latter three variables were not able to be proven in my study, not because they actually do not contribute to a greater probability, but because the structure of the study was such that evidence was confounded. What do I mean by confounded? Let me explain. This study was only for people who had pain or loss of range of motion from surgery where materials were placed in the body. As such, I never gave words of knowledge for this condition. Instead I had a strong measure of faith, if not a gift of faith, for healing of this condition. Yet, the last thirty-two years of ministry have proven to me by the overall experience in my meetings that words of knowledge do have a dramatic impact upon the probability of healing. Because there were no words of knowledge preceding the prayer for people with surgically implanted materials, the structure of the study made it impossible to verify the impact of words of knowledge for the healing of pain and mobility from surgically implanted materials.

In like manner, the only type of prayer I used from the platform when praying for healing of this condition were commanding prayers. Therefore, there was no way to compare the effects of commanding prayers to the effects of petitionary prayers. The structure of the study confounded the ability to prove this variable, whether or not commanding prayer was more effective than petitionary prayer.

The final variable that was confounded was the person's expectation of healing. This was confounded by the fact that people were healed who had little to no expectation of healing in the study. Sometimes they came with no expectation, but due to the events occurring in the meeting, though they had come without expectation, they developed expectation while in the meeting. There were others who were healed who did not come with expectation of being healed, and didn't have expectation of healing when they were healed. This created confusion in the survey regarding how to answer the question.

WHAT I DISCOVERED FROM MY STUDY

In science there is the understanding that you cannot prove something; you can only disprove something. This is based on the assumption that what you think you have proved could later be disproved by someone else. With this consideration the first assumption or belief I wanted to disprove was the belief of some that no one was being healed in my meetings. This I was easily able to disprove.

Though I had been ministering to people with loss of range of motion and/or pain from surgeries involving implanted materials from 2009 to this day, and continue to do so, the study was limited to 2012. During this year, when people reported their pain was reduced by at least 80 percent or their movement was restored by at least 80 percent, there were three times that information was taken: first, at the occasion of the reported healing; second, ten to fourteen days after the reported healing, to see if the healing had persisted; and third, one hundred–plus days after the initial report of healing.

Few people would have the degree of opportunity to study the occasions of healing and the numbers of healings on the scale that I had opportunity to investigate. By combining surveys with open-ended interviews, as well as case studies and field notes, I was able to create a body of evidence that demonstrates that people experienced healing.

Based on the study, it was discovered that about 50 percent of the time the person who received healing experienced some sensation before the healing. Often the person felt heat, and/or an electrical energy in the body before the manifestation of healing. The other 50 percent who were healed, however, did not experience such phenomena before the manifestation of their healing. These percentages were for all types of healings, and in some meetings, closer to 60 to 70 percent of the time there were physical manifestations or phenomena before the healing. However, when it came to the healing of pain and movement restriction due to surgically implanted material, the persons experienced these manifestations 90 percent of the time—especially heat or energy. This was much higher than for other types of healings. Further details for the methodology used for this study are available from the doctoral thesis.[3]

What were the results of this study? First, some assumptions of what the outcomes would be proved false. For example, I expected Brazil to have the highest success rate for healing, followed by Asia, then the United States, and the lowest results to come from Europe. This proved to be a wrong assumption. The following chart explains the results better. Hong Kong had the highest, with 86 percent healed. Australia was second, with 50 percent healed. Most shocking was Denmark, specifically Copenhagen, one of the most secularized cities in Europe, which was third highest in healings, with 44 percent healed. Another European country, the United Kingdom was fourth, with 41 percent healed. Brazil and Korea came in fifth and sixth, with each reporting 36 percent healed, and last was the United States, with 35 percent healed.

When the numbers of people reporting was factored in, however, it became obvious that when there were greater numbers studied in the respective countries, it appeared as if the greater the number studied in the countries, the lower the percentages. This was reflected in the fact that by far the countries that had the largest number of persons studied were Brazil and the United States.

When, instead of studying whole countries, individual churches were studied, the statistics regarding healing changed. Churches in Hong Kong, Singapore, and two churches in Australia all had two out of two healed. Brazil also reported 100 percent healed, with five out of five. The Brazilian church was a Baptist church.

Looking at the summary of the statistics, there were a total of 795 people involved in the study. Of these 795, 396 reported that their surgeries had not been successful, resulting in pain or loss of range of motion following the surgeries. A total of 149 of these 396 who needed healing and who could recognize if healing occurred by either pain reduction or increased range of motion reported that either one or both had improved by at least 80 percent. This resulted in 37.62 percent, almost 38 percent of those in the study who needed healing being healed significantly.

The following table gives more details.

TABLE 1. PERCENTAGE OF PEOPLE HEALED FROM SIM IN 2012

Location	Date	# of Persons with SIM	# of SIM Persons with Pain & ROM	# of Persons Healed	Healed (in %)
Master's Touch Intl. Church, Florida, USA	02/23/12	11	5	2	40%
Igreja Videira, Brazil	03/26/12	12	8	4	50%
Igreja Videira, Brazil	03/27/12	16	11	9	82%
Cultural Center, Denmark	04/26/12	20	9	1	11%
Cultural Center, Denmark	04/28/12	21	9	7	78%
Holy Trinity Swiss Cottage, England	05/01/12	16	8	1	13%
Edinburgh, Scotland	05/02/12	10	5	1	20%
Crossroads Church, Illinois, USA	05/29/12	24	11	8	73%
Revival Christian Church, Hong Kong	06/08/12	8	4	2	50%
Revival Christian Church, Hong Kong	06/09/12	6	3	2	67%
The Vine Church, Hong Kong	06/10/12	2	1	2	100%
WLI Conference, Korea	06/11/12	10	5	1	20%
Daegu Full Gospel, Church, Korea	06/15/12	5	2	2	100%

Location	Date	# of Persons with SIM	# of SIM Persons with Pain & ROM	# of Persons Healed	Healed (in %)
Daegu Full Gospel Church, Korea	06/16/12	10	5	1	20%
Shekinah Glory Church, Tennessee, USA	06/19/12	6	3	1	33%
New Life City, New Mexico, USA	06/21/12	31	15	2	13%
Ministério Internacional, Brazil	06/30/12	5	3	1	33%
Igreja Batista Evangélica, Brazil	07/01/12	5	3	1	33%
Igreja Batista Nova Canaã, Brazil	07/02/12	8	5	5	100%
Katie Souza Conference, Arizona, USA	07/13/12	20	9	5	56%
Churchlands Church, Australia	08/09/12	4	2	1	50%
Churchlands Church, Australia	08/10/12	4	2	2	100%
Kenmore Baptist Church, Australia	08/11/12	28	13	4	31%
Dayspring Church, Australia	08/17/12	4	2	2	100%
Catch the Fire Conference, England	08/31/12	32	15	7	50%
Catch the Fire Conference, England	09/01/12	9	4	3	75%
Holy Trinity Brompton, England	09/02/12	11	5	2	40%
Heartland Assembly, Iowa, USA	09/13/12	14	7	2	29%
Elim Fellowship, New York, USA	09/21/12	33	21	8	38%

Location	Date	# of Persons with SIM	# of SIM Persons with Pain & ROM	# of Persons Healed	Healed (in %)
Plentitude Igreja Em Células, Brazil	09/25/12	21	13	4	31%
Logos Church, Brazil	09/26/12	24	17	3	19%
Logos Church, Brazil	09/27/12	13	8	1	13%
Comunidade Cristá de Ribeirão Preta, Brazil	10/01/12	40	17	2	12%
Comunidade Cristá de Ribeirão Preta, Brazil	10/04/12	36	28	9	32%
Shalom Communidade Cristá, Brazil	10/05/12	19	18	9	50%
Evangel Church, Kentucky, USA	10/21/12	33	13	2	15%
Urbana Vineyard Church, Illinois, USA	11/03/12	61	27	11	41%
Awakened to Destiny, Colorado, USA	11/08/12	83	34	9	26%
WLI Conference, California, USA	11/16/12	11	7	3	43%
Apostolic Resource Center, Pennsylvania, USA	11/28/12	25	7	1	14%
Igreja Batista Água Viva, Brazil	12/09/12	27	14	4	29%
East Gate Church, Pennsylvania, USA	12/15/12	17	8	2	25%
Total		**795**	**406**	**149**	
Mean		**19**	**10**	**4**	**40%**

In addition to the quantitative study above, there was also a qualitative study made of twelve people. An in-depth open-ended interview was used with these twelve. Utilizing what is known in the medical field as the *visual analogy scale*, which is used especially within the physical therapy field to note the degree of healing immediately after the healing was reported, ten to fourteen days after, and one hundred–plus days later, the following chart reports the outcome of these twelve people regarding their pain levels.

TABLE 2. CHANGE IN PAIN LEVELS

Name	Before Healing	Immediately After Healing	100 Days After Healing
Abigail	4	0	0
Anne	10	1	3
Craig	8	0	0
Daryl	6	4	0
Diane	4–6	2	0
Greg	8	1	0
Jane	7	4	1
Lester	6	0	0
Michelle	7	2	2
Rachel	4	1	0
Robert	7	2	0
Ruth	5	0	0

Seven of the twelve studied had not only pain but range-of-motion issues. They reported the following. (ROM stands for range of motion.)

TABLE 3. CHANGE IN RANGE OF MOTION

Name*	Length of loss of ROM	Before Healing	After Healing
Abigail	N/A	N/A	N/A
Anne	1.5 years	Could not run or bend ankle at certain angle	Can run, squat, go up and down stairs, dance
Craig	2 years	Could not lift shoulder above head	Able to wave arms above head

Name*	Length of loss of ROM	Before Healing	After Healing
Daryl	N/A	Ankle turned 45 degrees in when walking	Can walk without problem now
Diane	17 years	Could not flex or twist to the side easily	Able to move without pain
Jane	10 years	Could not go up and down stairs without assistance	Can jog up and down stairs
Lester	Since age 21	Could not bend over	Can now bend down and tie shoes
Ruth	N/A	Could not feel chin or lips	Can now feel sensation on lips

*Table only includes participants who went through in-depth interview and had range-of-motion issues before their healing.

SUMMARY OF MY STUDY

It is noteworthy that no systematic studies of any type of Christian intercessory prayer for divine healing of surgically implanted materials have been published in the religious or scientific literature. Even if a more general subject, such as interventions for chronic lower back pain (with or without prior surgery involving surgically implanted materials), was studied, there were minimal effects attributed to complementary and alternative medicine, CAM. In October 2007, a meta-analysis of all traditional medical and CAM therapies for chronic low back pain was published in the *Annals of Internal Medicine*. The authors tabulated all known studies found in the Cochrane Database of Systemic Reviews and MEDLINE, a journal citation database, up until November 2006, and they established a therapy as having "good evidence" for positive outcomes if the average patient improved one to two points on the ten-point visual analog scale—10–20 percent.

Cognitive-behavioral therapy, exercise, spinal manipulation, and interdisciplinary rehabilitation had good evidence (a one- to two-point increase in improvement), but other CAM measures, such as acupuncture, massage, and yoga, did not rise to this one- to two-point level. Prayer was not included in this study.[4]

When the results of my study are compared with those in the *Annals of Internal Medicine*, there is reason to be greatly encouraged by the efficacy of Christian prayer. Instead of moving one or two points on the ten-point visual analog scale, the ones self-reporting among the participants in this study indicated an average six-point improvement. When the respondents in this study were re-interviewed after ten days and then after one hundred days, their average improvement in pain greatly exceeded the threshold of a one- or two-point improvement on the visual analog scale. After one hundred days, of the twelve who were re-interviewed, two participants had improved four points, another had improved four to six points, one had improved five points, two had improved six points, one had improved seven points, and two had improved eight points, all of whom had 100 percent improvement. The other participants improved five, six, and seven points, respectively, with the average improvement being six points. These results are quite remarkable and show the need for future studies to demonstrate the efficacy of Christian prayer, such as platform commanding prayer, or another type of prayer, proximity intercessory prayer, for these conditions.

My research model went through varying stages before it concluded with a workable questionnaire and interview combination. While I did not necessarily determine that I could predict who would be healed in any given meeting, I was able to discover certain factors that may affect healing. For example, the research showed that some of the six variables I studied, including a personal theology of healing, training on healing, and previous experience with healing, had a positive effect on a person's probability of being healed.

Continued research and follow-up with those claiming that metal disappeared is needed to verify more conclusive and concrete results. I was neither able to confirm or disprove these claims in my study. However, since 2009 I have been witnessing reports of healing from pain and/or decrease of range of motion from surgeries with surgically implanted materials. This research showed that not only were people healed at the time of the meeting, but they also remained healed one hundred days or more after the healing, continuing to live with less pain and more mobility, sometimes after years of experiencing difficulty. These findings are clearly extraordinary given the state of the research on pain therapies against which this research began. It is also important to realize the placebo effect is not a good, viable explanation for the healings.

CHAPTER 12

HEALING AND THE PLACEBO EFFECT

Realizing that some may attempt to explain the results of my thesis as being due to the placebo effect rather than to a supernatural source, it is important to consider this issue more thoroughly. The reasons for interpreting all healings and miracles as due to the placebo effect is to misunderstand what is happening—it fails to account for the fact that the placebo effect is controversial within the field of medicine and has become, along with spontaneous remission, the naturalistic explanation for the work of God or the power of faith.[1]

The placebo effect is closely related to the issue of faith, and the question raised by Dr. Herbert Benson, professor of medicine at Harvard Medical School, "Has God hardwired our bodies for faith?" would be answered "Yes!" God has hardwired our bodies to respond to faith. And in a much greater way than Dr. Benson would accept or believe. Dr. Benson would not allow for a supernatural interpretation of the placebo effect, relegating it to and explaining it purely on naturalistic terms.[2]

However, the placebo effect as medically understood is generally short-lived, and there is no evidence of the placebo effect in connection with lost range of motion being regained. The results of this study indicated the healing to be long-lived, and it affected not only the levels of pain, but also the range of motion.

Dr. Benson considers the placebo effect to be powerful and long lasting.[3] This is the opposite understanding of the placebo effect found in the Cochrane Report, which views it as weak and short-lived.[4] Furthermore, Benson did not think it was possible for the placebo effect to have a supernatural causation. Benson would not accept a testimony of improvements that were claimed to be miraculous. He would see the improvements mentioned in his book as the result of a mind-body-spirit connection, but the spirit would be the human spirit, never the Holy Spirit. Benson stated, "I do not believe it is possible to hover or to perform other physical feats that defy *Newtonian physics*. Do not get me wrong, the faith factor is a remarkable feature of *human physiology*. The mind is certainly capable of incredible influence, over physiology, as we've seen in the Tibetan monks in India."[5] This quote reveals that Benson is working within the old Newtonian, liberal, human construct rather than that of the invading kingdom of God, with its miraculous powers that supersede Newtonian physics.

Benson sees all faith in all religions to work on the same naturalistic principle of the placebo effect, which he renamed "remembered wellness."[6] He does not have a supernaturalistic understanding of the benefits of faith as a result of a theistic God acting in human history. Benson believes remembered wellness is at work in therapeutic touch.[7] Benson further reveals his understanding of faith healing as being a form of self-healing by stating, "But in this book, I am emphasizing confidence in and admiration for one's *internal healing resources* in hopes that we can strike a better balance between what caregivers give us or do for us—medicines and procedures—and the underappreciated role of *self-care*."[8]

Benson noted that based on studies thus far, he has not found healing through faith to be demonstrated to be caused by divine intervention. But he appears open to this possibility in the following statement: "Despite the lack of confirmation or consensus in these studies of faith healing, we know from the previously mentioned experiments on remembered wellness that a caregiver's beliefs can empower healing. Yet we must further study faith healing if we are to credit it for benefits over and above that of remembered wellness."[9]

As indicated above, however, this openness excludes anything that would conflict with Newtonian physics. Hence, divine healing, when understood as supernatural or miraculous, has been ruled out of Benson's interpretation a priori. This is an example of why we spent time discussing and explaining the role of Enlightenment thinking in modern historiography, medicine, philosophy, and theology. Consequently, such a narrow frame of interpretation is unable to explain the relevant evidence of improvements associated with Christian prayer, which are dramatically more pronounced than those published in previous studies of pain therapy.

THE NATURALISTIC EXPLANATION OF HEALING AND MIRACLES AS THE PLACEBO EFFECT

There are three reasons for rejecting the naturalistic explanations, including the placebo effect, as the only explanations for healing. The first is the surprise healings—even of mockers and critics—that have occurred in Global Awakening's meetings. The second reason is that the internal body-mind-spirit mechanism could clearly not be used as the explanation for certain types of healings or miracles. This is true for the phenomenon of the raising of the dead, especially where those who have been raised from the dead were dead for more than an hour. Third are the inconsistent prayer results where one person prays for different people. This one person might pray for ten people and see nothing happen to six, while two receive complete healing, and two receive partial healings, as an example. This causes one to recognize that healing is not dependent upon him or her, but upon the power or energy of God that works through him or her, although not necessarily on a consistent basis. The following section will further detail these three reasons.

Surprise healings of persons who did not expect healing, in some cases did not believe in healing through prayers in Jesus' name, and sometimes came to mock and criticize the meetings, contradict the understanding of the mental state of so-called remembered wellness required for the placebo effect to work.[10] This occurred in a meeting conducted in Colorado. The sister of a chiropractor came to the meeting to criticize and mock Global Awakening's ministry at a Global School of Healing and Impartation. While standing in the back, she was suddenly healed. The woman's brother, who was a believer, shared this story with me a few days after the healing occurred.

The second reason for rejecting a naturalistic interpretation of the placebo effect is the raising of the dead through prayer in Jesus' name. I have met several people who reported that they were raised from the dead, interviewed their families to confirm their reports of being raised from the dead, and visited the villages that were once Muslim but are now predominantly Christian because the villagers confirmed the report of those who were raised from the dead. After interviewing the humble people whom God used to raise the dead, and after seeing the effect on a nation such as Mozambique, where ten thousand new churches were started and one million people accepted Jesus due, in part, to healings and miracles, especially the dead who were raised, a naturalistic explanation of faith as a placebo will simply not suffice to explain all the relevant evidence.

A third reason for rejecting a naturalistic interpretation of the placebo effect stems from the inconsistent healing among those who experience healing. For example, two brothers came for prayer in a meeting in southern India. Neither was able to walk due to the same condition in their legs. One was healed, while the other had no improvement. There may have been a difference in expectation on the part of each brother, but no one could really know the inner workings of their minds regarding their expectations concerning healing. In this case, however, I believe that what was most important was the faith of the person ministering. Many times, it is not the faith of the person in need of healing that determines whether a healing occurs, as both brothers were Hindus, but it is the faith of the person ministering that often is determinative. The point is that the level of faith was the same—actually it was higher after the one brother was healed that the second brother would be healed. He was not healed. If there would have been a right atmosphere to enhance the possibility of a placebo effect, this would have been that atmosphere, for both the unhealed brother and for me, the one who had prayed for both boys' healing.

Another example of this inconsistency dates back to 1984. John Wimber had allowed me to shadow him at several healing meetings. The instruction was to watch and listen and, at the end of the meeting, ask him any questions from what was observed. One night, at a Methodist church in Houston, almost every person John prayed for was healed. The following night nobody was healed who John prayed for. At the end of the second night, I said, "John, I have a question," to which he responded, "Let me tell you what your question is. You want to know why everyone was healed last night and no one was healed tonight, don't you?"

I said, "Yes."

John asked, "You don't get it, do you? Last night, when everyone I prayed for was healed, I didn't go to bed thinking I was some great healer; that I was somebody. And tonight when I go to bed, I am not going to be thinking I am a great failure. I didn't have any more faith last night than I did tonight, and I don't have any more sin in my life tonight than I did last night. Tomorrow I will get up and pray for the sick again. All I did both nights was stick my fat hand out and say, 'Come, Holy Spirit.'"

This dialogue with John was a turning point. The answer to a breakthrough in healing was not some secret to be learned. Neither was it based on the merit of the person praying. It was wrapped in mystery, but related to faithfulness and to being willing to persevere in ministering God's love to those in need of healing. This does not negate the purpose of this study—to disprove the null hypothesis that no one was being healed, or the secondary purpose of trying to determine if there are independent variables that influence the probability of people being healed. Those questions have been answered. The 149 persons who reported having been healed from complications involving surgically implanted material in 2012 disproved the null hypothesis, and this only referred to the one type of condition that was being studied. There were thousands more who reported having been healed of numerous other diseases, including terminal cancer. (Spontaneous remission is supposed to be an anomaly, with one out of sixty thousand to one out of a hundred thousand, but the ones healed of cancer in Global Awakening's ministry is an anomaly of the anomaly, with a much higher probability than the standard anomaly.) These results question a purely naturalistic explanation of the placebo effect, which for some in the scientific or medical field becomes synonymous with faith.

Another area that affects the issue of inconsistency is the difference between the evangelistic context and the pastoral context of the ministry of healing. If the placebo effect were the naturalistic explanation for healing, then why is it that when the gospel is declared through a demonstration of healing, where non-Christians are being asked to become followers of Jesus, the percentage of those healed is much higher than in a pastoral context?

This would appear to contradict the variables in this study. In the missiological context, non-Christians often have not heard the gospel, know nothing about the Christian faith other than that it is not their faith, have not previously seen anyone healed in Jesus' name, and have no theology of healing. Why do more people get healed in this context than in what would seem to be a more conducive atmosphere of a Christian church service in a denomination that believes in healing, where the people have heard of testimonies of people they know personally who were healed, and where there has been a building of faith through teaching solid biblical teachings regarding healing?

The answer appears to be the overriding desire of God to advance His kingdom through salvation, which includes healing. For example, the greatest number of conversions I have seen in one meeting was in India. There was a gathering of one hundred thousand persons, mostly Hindus. Based on an estimated number of those waving their hands, indicating their healing of at least 80 percent, approximately fifty thousand of these were healed in one night, and thirty thousand accepted Jesus.

This example begs the question of sovereignty in relation to healing, but it also relates sovereignty to soteriology (the study of salvation). Though healing is wrapped in mystery, some things are beginning to be better understood as one seeks to better understand the "ways of God."[11] Perhaps God has determined to link healing to the gospel, intentionally making healing a sign to confirm the gospel, or—more accurately and biblically—perhaps healing is part of the gospel, and is included in the good news that Jesus bore our sins, sicknesses, and sorrows on the cross.

Indeed, the energy of the kingdom of God has broken into this time and space, and the energy of heaven has begun to come to earth.

CHAPTER 13

ENERGY AND A CASE FOR MIRACLES

A s one better understands the ways of God, one will experience more of the energy of God. The issue of the energy of God is key to this study. Reiki, therapeutic touch, and other energy healing modalities, including prayer, are listed on the website of the National Institutes of Health as complementary and alternative medical treatments.[1]

There are four possible explanations for the source of energy that is often experienced by people who report healing. First is a naturalistic explanation that asserts that the energy is either innate to the human body, or due to the placebo effect, or the result of love or affection. The second possible explanation is that the energy is part of the cosmos, and people can learn to channel this energy, especially healers, such as shamans, spiritists, spiritualists, Jewish rabbis, Muslim mullahs, Hindu pundits, or Christian pastors or priests. This New Age perspective is tied to a belief in pantheism—that all is one, and that there is no distinction between God and creation.[2] In this view, God becomes more of an impersonal force that is part of the universe. All major theistic world religions, such as Islam, Judaism, and Christianity, would take issue with this view, because these religions believe in a personal God as a creator.

A third possible explanation for the source of energy is the theistic derstanding that God is distinct from creation, as its creator. In this view, there are two energy sources: angelic energy, from both holy and fallen angels, and the energy of God experienced in the immanence of God, especially through His gifts, which are manifestations of His energies. These are communicated by the Holy Spirit. This view rests upon a two-kingdoms-in-conflict perspective

Finally, the fourth view, which is the view I embrace, is a synthesis of the first and the third views, while rejecting the second, or pantheistic New Age view. Following are additional details on each of the four mentioned explanations.

THE NATURALISTIC EXPLANATION OF ENERGY SOURCES: HUMAN ENERGY

The naturalistic understanding of energy explains the feeling of energy by changes in the processes of the brain, which has been proven by modern science. This is how the placebo effect is understood. It has no reference to the human spirit, which would move the discussion beyond the naturalistic explanation or the scientific explanation.

A variation of this naturalistic explanation is to allow the existence of the human spirit. This view would see the human spirit as natural, and not supernatural. The feeling of heat or energy or some other phenomenon would be viewed as rooted in the human spirit. The human spirit would be considered to be either one with the Spirit of the One, without distinction, or separate. The human spirit in this understanding is created and has a degree of power unto itself. The former understanding of the human spirit (one with the Spirit of the One) would be more suitable to a pantheistic worldview, and the latter (one separate from the Holy Spirit of a personal God) to a theistic worldview. The earlier discussion of the human spirit would be more suitable to a purely naturalistic, atheistic worldview. I believe in the latter view of the human spirit as created and separate from God, yet there is a means by which communication with God is possible.[3]

THE PANTHEISTIC, NEW AGE ENERGY EXPLANATION OF ENERGY SOURCES

The pantheistic view of energy would see many of the world religions' understanding of power as the same. Whether it is called "ki," "chi," "prana," or "Odic force," or some other name for a "universal life force," it is all the same energy of the One.[4] This is the New Age understanding that is similar to the understanding of healing in Reiki, therapeutic touch, healing touch, and shamanism. In this view, god is not a personal god, but more the impersonal "ground of all being."[5]

This understanding is inconsistent with the traditional theistic worldview. The Catholic Church clearly rejects this view and considers energy-healing modalities as potential open doors to the demonic. It views an attempt to manipulate or control healing energy apart from Christ as sorcery or occult magic.[6]

THE THEISTIC, TWO-KINGDOM UNDERSTANDING OF ENERGY SOURCES

Theism does not require a two-kingdoms-at-war worldview. Some scholars would think such a two-kingdom view threatens the understanding of God's sovereignty. However, this worldview does appear to be the backdrop of much of the New Testament.[7] It is not complete dualism, but rather a modified dualistic viewpoint that is subsumed under the belief that there is no question who wins the war—God is sovereign, and the kingdoms on this earth will become the kingdom of His Christ.[8]

In this two-kingdoms-at-war worldview, there is a personified devil, and he rules over a demonic kingdom of demonic spirits. These principalities, powers, and demons have a degree of power (energy) that is part of their created order. Although Lucifer's fall has corrupted this power, his kingdom of demonic spirits still maintains the power given to them in creation. However, they can no longer go into the full presence of God (Rev. 4:2) except for a limited appearance in His heavenly courtroom (1 Kings 22:19–22; Job 1:6–12; 2:1–7; Ps. 82:1; Zech. 3:1–5). This is significant because both humans and angelic beings have the capacity to be anointed (energized) beyond the power of their created order with that order's innate energy. This energizing or anointing takes place through the presence of God. This means the power of the fallen angelic beings is not as strong as the power of those that did not fall, because the fallen angels cannot go into God's full presence to be filled with His glory and power, which is beyond that of their created order, innate to them.

The angelic power for those who did not fall is not limited to that which is innate to their created order, because they can ascend and descend, or come into and go out from heaven's realm. This allows them, just as those believers who are in Christ, to be energized, or anointed, by the Holy Spirit.[9]

Even if the above interpretation of anointing related to the angelic is discounted, it still remains that they have power, both the fallen and the holy angels, and they are active in human affairs.[10] The Holy Spirit is the ultimate power, which is immensely greater than the limited power of angels or humans. Only God is omnipotent, while His created orders of beings are not. God makes His power known through the Holy Spirit. The gifts of the Holy Spirit are manifestations of His energies.[11]

One should not redefine the Holy Spirit's power with a pantheistic understanding of God, let alone call it the "spirit of Reiki," as Ruth Mayeux Allen refers to it in her book, *The Holy Spirit and the Spirit of Reiki.*[12] I believe this view is deceptive and is rooted in a view of Jesus that John, the writer of 1 John in the Christian Bible, would consider a teaching from the spirit of antichrist.[13]

HEALING AND ENERGY: A SYNTHESIS ROOTED IN THE THEISTIC VIEW

There exists another view of the source of the energy for healing, which represents a synthesis based on an acceptance of the power of the human spirit, the power of angelic spirits (both fallen and non-fallen), and the power of the Holy Spirit as understood in the traditional theistic view. I believe that the degree of power that was innate to human beings was diminished in the fall, as well as the authority of human beings in relation to God. In addition, the *imago Dei* (image of God) was marred (Brunner), not destroyed (Barth).[14] Because it was not destroyed, the power of the human spirit, which was made in the image of God, retained power, but because it was marred, the human spirit did not retain as much power as before the fall.

As a result, healing can occur from this power of the human spirit without necessitating a supernatural or other spiritual explanation. Some of the low-grade healings reported in medical studies, such as healing of anxiety, headaches, pain reduction of lower-pain thresholds, and minor psychosomatic healings can be explained from this perspective. Much of what Benson attributes to the placebo effect would fall in this category. Some of the healings reported by twentieth-century English theologian Leslie D. Weatherhead in his book *Psychology, Religion, and Healing,* and his later book, *Wounded Spirits,* could also be explained in this manner.[15] This may include some of the effects of those ministering with ki, chi, prana, Odic force, and other names for what is otherwise referred to as the universal life force.

This is where things become troublesome. It is sometimes difficult to determine when the agent of healing behind the healing is the human spirit and when it moves over to the occult area of healing through fallen angels, referred to in Reiki, healing touch, and therapeutic touch as "spirit guides."[16] I believe that these "spirit guides" are no longer part of the human spirit category but part of the angelic spirit category. One of the disconcerting aspects of the New Age religion is the lack of discernment regarding these angelic spirits or spirit guides. There is the tendency to think they are all positive and good, without belief in fallen angels or the demonic. In this way, many people open themselves up to the demonic.[17]

As previously stated, most Christian scholars view demonic spirits as fallen angels. "Angelic spirits" are angels of God who did not follow Lucifer, and thus did not fall from their heavenly position. They can be anointed by the power of the Holy Spirit, and are therefore more powerful than demonic angelic beings. Again, they outnumber the fallen angels by two to one. They not only have the degree of power and glory God assigned to them in their creation, but they can carry His glory and power (Ps. 18:9–10; Isa. 6:1–7; Ezek. 1:4–23; 10:2–20; Rev. 4:6–8). Until Christians receive their glorified bodies, they cannot experience as much of the energy, power, and glory of God as the angels can. The reason for this is that human beings cannot stand the energy; it causes them to fall under the power of God, or to experience so much electricity that they fear death from the power.[18]

Greater than the power of the human spirit and greater than the power of the angelic spirits is the power of the Holy Spirit, the person of the Trinity who reveals the immanence of God. Since the members of the Trinity have coequality in all things, the Holy Spirit is omnipresent, omniscient, and omnipotent.[19]

I am proposing that the energies involved in Christian healing, non-Christian healing, and naturalistic healing are not necessarily the same. The view of the energy coming from the One, and people having the ability to learn to channel this energy, I strongly reject. This pantheistic understanding of reality is in conflict with the understanding of the reality of God in theistic religions, including Christianity, Judaism, and Islam. I believe the energy of the human spirit can heal minor sicknesses and that it is neither good nor bad, but neutral.[20] Greater healing can come from the angelic realm, with even greater healing coming from the holy angels than the fallen ones. This is because the holy angels can also carry the energy of the Holy Spirit (Dan. 10:18; Luke 22:43), as can Christians.[21] Perhaps this is why the Bible describes the angels as ascending and descending the ladder or stairway from heaven, or upon Jesus (Gen. 28:12; John 1:51). The angels have come to serve those who have eternal life,[22] and are now returning to receive a fresh anointing or energy from God by being in His presence.[23]

This reflection does not demonize all forms of healing that are not done in the name of Jesus, because it allows for the neutral type of healing that is related to the human spirit and that is not drawing upon other spiritual powers. Therapeutic touch cofounders Dolores Krieger and Dora Kunz give instructions to call upon spirit guides—angelic beings.[24] It is clear, however, that they do not view these angelic beings from a biblical perspective; rather, they are impersonal forces or energies. Thus, there is grave danger that the angel is a fallen, unholy angel and a person could become demonized by calling upon these spirit guides.[25]

Krieger and Kunz's belief that whether or not someone is healed can depend upon his or her karma is disconcerting, because one of the obstacles to people receiving healing is the feeling that they are unworthy of healing due to how they have lived their lives, or that they have brought this sickness, disease, or condition upon themselves by their lifestyles.[26] This is where the message of *grace* is more powerful than the message of *karma*.[27]

I have seen all three types of healings occur in my meetings: healing through the human spirit, healing through holy angelic spirits, and healing through the Holy Spirit. Miracles are always dependent upon a strong anointing of the Holy Spirit, and often it is the gifts of the Holy Spirit that cause the faith of the individual who is praying, the one being prayed for, or both to experience the *faith of God—the mountain-moving faith—the gift of faith.*[28]

Concerning the powers of darkness and the powers of light, one might ask how so much evil could ever take place on earth. The more serious issues do not deal with the power of a single demon, power, or principality. The danger is when these evil personalities gain control over humans—over their minds and their wills—and begin to use them as mere puppets in the grand schemes of Satan—for example, when Satan used his deceptive powers that were represented in Nazism, fascism, Communism, ethnic cleansings, religious wars, drug cartel wars, and the Khmer People's Revolutionary Army, to name a few. These are truly the most dangerous ways evil incarnates itself in the ways of humans.

Hundreds of millions of lives have been lost due to the philosophies of demons that became politicized and were empowered by the cruel power wielded by humans against other humans in the form of war, pillage, and oppression. Millions more have lost their lives due to nationalistic or political wars than in the religious wars mentioned earlier. These nationalistic or political wars were rooted in the philosophical writings of the Enlightenment that influenced Nazism and Communism.

It is not the personal sins of individuals that have brought so much tragedy to the human race; it is the structural power of evil through the philosophy of demons. Therefore, society needs well-trained philosophers and theologians who can spot and speak out against this potential terrible evil. The church's attempt to confront this structural evil through "liberation theology" has been a failure.[29]

WHY BOTHER WITH TRYING TO
VERIFY HEALINGS? WHY BOTHER TO
MAKE A CASE FOR MIRACLES?

I have had great concern that the Christian church realized its need to verify the results of prayer in Jesus' name based on case studies. A few years ago, I providentially found a copy of a talk by the cofounder of therapeutic touch, Dora Kunz, in which she stated that Christians did not take the time to verify the healings in their ministries.[30] She had just come from a meeting of Christian healing ministries in which she was the only "heathen" (her word).[31]

In her talk, she noted that the medical profession wanted to see the records of the healings to verify the healings, but almost none of the Christian healing ministers were supplying any records, with the exception of Leslie Weatherhead, the Methodist minister from London, who had meticulously kept records of the cases they were working with. Dora Kunz lamented:

> That is the one thing that all the doctors and psychiatrists who attended all these Conferences are begging for. They are begging for medical reports to be kept, and I've got to admit that practically not one of them [Christian healing ministers] does it. This doctor Leslie Weatherhead in England who is the head of some big Methodist church in London, is the only one who, you might say, has the scientific mind and a scientific method of keeping constantly records, year by year. The rest of them are[,] well[,] they are so busy, they do not have the time. They say[,] we come and we try to help people because we are asked and we cannot be bothered to take records. They are definitely, I think, on the defensive a little bit and that is, of course, the one thing everyone is begging for, the records.[32]

Later, therapeutic touch would develop, with Kunz and Dolores Krieger as the original cofounders. They realized the importance of keeping records and making case studies. This has given them legitimacy within the medical profession and with some insurance companies. Christian ministers and ministries are now playing catch up.

It is important to keep records for verification within the medical community and the insurance companies. In October 2010, at the largest annual conference of Global Awakening, a vision was presented that outlined the need to work with the medical community to verify the healings that were occurring in Global Awakening's ministry, but not just Global Awakening's ministry—any Christian ministry that had records of healing in Jesus' name. The vision was presented at a special meeting for people in the medical field. By the following annual conference, others had caught the vision.

Dr. Martin Moore-Ede, a former professor of Harvard Medical School, decided to help develop an entity for the purpose of medical verification of cures, and for developing case studies that follow medical protocol and comply with medical practice for publication of research studies.

The original group of people from this meeting would later comprise the board of directors: Drs. Martin and Donna Moore-Ede; Drs. Joshua and Candy Brown; and Dr. Brenda Jones. They worked with Global Awakening to form a nonprofit organization independent from Global Awakening. The name of this nonprofit was Global Medical Research Institute.

As of August 2017, the board of directors consisted of Joshua Brown, PhD; Candy Gunther Brown, PhD; Brenda Jones, PhD, MSN, CNM-BC, FNP-BC; and David Zaritzky, MD.

Therapeutic touch and Reiki practitioners have been able to charge some insurance companies for their ministry to the sick;

however, to the best of my knowledge, no Christian ministries of healing have been able to receive insurance payments for their ministry of healing in the hospitals and clinics. Why? As pointed out by Dora Kunz, therapeutic touch has understood the importance of medical verification, giving it legitimacy in the eyes of the medical field. Another reason is they created a certification training program for therapeutic touch. I was told Christians did not have a certification program for training in healing. It was to answer this situation that I created the Christian Healing Certification Program. I am not asking for Christianity to have a favored position, just an equal access and equal opportunity.

CHAPTER 14

MOUNT CARMEL AND THE COMING END-TIMES REVIVAL

The title of this chapter contains the secret to evangelism in these last days—power evangelism. You see, it was at Mount Carmel that a confrontation between the powers took place—the powers of evil versus the Power of God—and the result of this confrontation was a wholesale return to God: a "revival."

The Bible is full of confrontation. And as it was in the beginning, so it shall be in the end. As we get closer to the end of this age, there will be increased warfare between the kingdom of God and the kingdoms of this world. Specifically, there will be warfare between the power of God and the "powers" of evil.[1] According to one New Testament scholar, since the Bible actually says that Jesus Christ is the end, we have been in the last days since He came. Obviously, we are in the latter part of the last days now, and many things are taking place, and there are more to come. There will be an increase in wickedness and power, both in the church and in the enemy camp, in the last days. There will also be an increase in healing, miracles, signs, and wonders. Some will be "lying wonders," performed in an effort to deceive the saints (see 2 Thess. 2:9 KJV), but there will also be genuine greater signs and wonders in the church than have ever been seen.

Now is the time to be strong in the Lord and strong in your faith!

150

So, what is faith? How do we demonstrate it? All the way through the narratives in the Bible, we see that faith is hearing God for oneself—and obeying. That is faith. When you obey what God tells you to do, the word God gave you will be tested. It will not be easy to do what He calls you to do; His command will be opposed, because you are going into the enemy camp, but you must do it anyway. God will lead you. He speaks to you, and subtly He moves you. Learn to recognize the move and the voice of God. Most of us hear the whisper of God. We've got to tune ourselves to it, because sometimes when He speaks, we don't know to listen, but God likes to talk to us, and He loves when we respond to Him in faith. He initiates faith by telling His children to do something. Listening, then having strength to obey, is the practice of faith. Faith isn't necessarily just what you believe. That is a part of it, but faith itself is biblically depicted as obedience to God's directives, not merely moral assent (see James 2:20–22). This pattern is very present throughout the Bible.[2] The following stories are illustrative of the battle over faith.

The first battle is between Moses and the sorcerers of Egypt (Ex. 7:9–12). We're talking some pretty heavy-duty occult stuff. The Egyptian sorcerers threw their staffs to the ground, which turned into serpents. Signs and wonders! But then Aaron's staff also turned into a serpent and swallowed theirs. The result? The people of Israel had the faith to follow Moses out of Egypt. By the time God sent the ten plagues—especially, the tenth plague, bringing death to all Egypt's firstborn—Pharaoh was glad to let them go (see Exodus 12). This was a power encounter between Pharaoh and God, because up to this time, the people believed that Pharaoh himself was a god. But God was going to show them who was *really* God, and He would do that by bringing His people out of Egypt.

The book of Exodus is quoted more in Revelation than in any

other book of the Bible. There is a correlation between the plagues in Revelation and the plagues in Egypt. Every time a plague came on the people of Egypt, God's people were protected in the midst of it. It didn't touch them. What saved them and brought healing to their bodies was eating the flesh of the lamb. When God brought Israel out of Egypt by His mighty hand, there was not one feeble person among them.[3] There had been supernatural healing. The blood of the lamb protected and saved them when the death angel passed over. Their lives were spared by the blood on their doorposts, symbolic of the blood of Jesus Christ. Every sick one, every feeble one, was healed that night when they ate the flesh. Likewise, we are healed when we partake of Christ. The prophet Isaiah, seven hundred years before Jesus was born, wrote that by His stripes we are healed, and that in His own body He bore our sickness and diseases (Isa. 53:4–5; cf. 53:11c, 12c).

God would always ask Moses to do weird things, irrational things that did not make sense. But they were opportunities for Moses to believe God and to exercise faith.

"You don't have water? Talk to a rock."

"You've got an army coming against you and the Red Sea behind you? Hold out your staff."

We read it, but we fail to realize what it would have been like in that time. God delighted in Moses because his obedience was faith. We need to understand that obedience is better than sacrifice. It is not enough to just come to church on Sunday and worship a little bit and then live our lives without obedience. As much as God loves worship, He would rather whisper to us and see if we will listen and obey. This is the most common biblical illustration of faith, and He wants us to be a faithful people. He wants an army of "lil' ole me's" who can hear and will obey His directives—and exercise faith. This is what the new covenant was meant to enable. We live in a breathtaking time; an exciting opportunity stands before us to believe God and participate in a great revival.

And a revival is coming. According to a popular prophecy of the 1980s,[4] the first wave will be among the church; the second wave will be on the streets. The Toronto Blessing, I believe, was a revival of renewal to the church, and next God will want to bring the lost in the revival in the streets. This is already occurring on the streets of Belfast and other towns in Great Britain; Copenhagen, Denmark; and other cities of the world. The last-days harvest of souls will be accomplished by our listening to God's individual whispers to us about someone's needs. The power of the Holy Spirit will come because we obeyed; and each act of obedience will release heaven's power, working through us—in signs and wonders—to bring the lost to repentance. *This* is power evangelism.[5]

Another illustration of faith's relationship to obedience is found in 1 Kings 18, where we read about Elijah and the 450 prophets of Baal. In this passage Elijah summoned the 450 false prophets to Mount Carmel. So wicked King Ahab sent word for the prophets to assemble there. Angrily, Elijah said to the onlookers, "How long will you waver between two opinions? If the LORD is God, follow him; but if Baal is God, follow him" (v. 21). I hope you are not wavering between two opinions in your life, trying to decide who you will follow—God or the *powers of this evil age.* God is jealous and will not share your affections with other gods. Mixing any other god with the true God brought much condemnation to Israel.

"Whoever is God will answer by fire," Elijah told the propets and the people gathered on the hillside. He had gotten that impression from a small voice. How hard would it have been to hear that voice and, by faith, act on it? Yet he did, and his obedience was faith.

Elijah built an altar of stone and laid a cut bull in pieces on the wood. Then he instructed that water be poured on the altar and on the wood on which the bull lay. Finally, Elijah prayed to God, a simple prayer reminding Him that he had done everything according to God's command. This is faith; obeying God. Then fire fell from heaven and burned the sacrifice, burned the wood, burned the stones. When all the people saw this, they fell down and cried, "The LORD, He is God!" (v. 39). This battle was won by Elijah's obedience to God's leading. He did what the 450 prophets of Baal could not do— called down fire from heaven—and this miracle turned the hearts of the people.

This is what will happen in the end times. We will not convince the world of the truth by our reasoned arguments; they will be convinced by the demonstration of God's power. A billion-soul harvest awaits the church. And it will be the power of God, demonstrated by His people, that will cause the world to believe the gospel of Christ. This is how countries were won in the first few centuries of the church. And, it will be the primary way they will be won in the last days before the coming of Christ. Let me illustrate with a story from my former pastorate.

I had a friend named Chuck in St. Louis who would go to coffee-houses that were gathering places for witches and warlocks and reveal the secrets of the hearts of those people. He had faith for this. He'd begin by saying, "You want to feel God?" Then he'd put his hand over theirs, but not touching them, and they would feel an almost-electric power touching their hands, often jumping back or emitting some expletive. "I told you, you would feel God," Chuck would say. He led more people to Jesus Christ and brought more people to my church than the rest of the church put together. He didn't use arguments; he used power. He got the power by hearing the Lord. He heard God by listening. He listened because He believed God would speak.

God wants to use you to bring glory to Him where you work. God wants to use you to bring glory to Him in your neighborhood and your family. He wants to give you prophecies for people, words of knowledge for healing, and He wants you to use the authority of His Son Jesus' name to cast out demons.

Today's Mount Carmel is the hospitals, the clinics, and among the medical community. The confrontation will be between those who believe in Jesus Christ and those who embrace Reiki, therapeutic touch, healing touch, and other "healing" techniques that are not of God. We must become more proficient in recognizing God's voice and having faith to do what He says. So much of what happens in healing results from hearing a word of knowledge. Hearing and seeing is not always literally hearing with our ears and seeing with our eyes; it is perceiving. God can use all your senses to speak to you. You simply have to learn His language, and how do you learn? You have to be willing to humble yourself and step out and see if you heard right. You'll only know if you obey and do what He said to do. After a while you can discern the difference between your ideas and God's voice.

Let's return to the Bible for another historical event that illustrates the battle between God and the occult forces. In Acts 8, a sorcerer named Simon came to the Lord through the evangelist Philip. For some time, Simon had practiced sorcery in the city. He had amazed the people with his magic and occult arts. But Philip came and demonstrated the power of God through signs and wonders, and the people paid attention. Many paralytics and cripples were healed. Then, when they heard Philip preach, they believed on the name of Jesus Christ, and Simon himself believed and was baptized. This guy had been the most powerful person working in demonic power in that city, yet when Philip showed up, Simon was astonished at the difference between the power of Jesus and the false power he had wielded. So, Simon made the decision to follow Jesus Christ, and there was great joy in the city of Samaria.

There is going to be a nameless, faceless revival. And when

stadiums fill, we will need thousands on the ministry team, and they will be trained and ready to go. We are talking about stadiums and the church being there with three thousand intercessors. By the time we start the meeting, people will already be healed. It will not be evangelism based on reason but on the power and Word of God. I have already experienced such stadium meetings in India, Brazil, and Argentina. It is now time for the Western world—North America and Europe—to take part. Power evangelism is biblical, and this is where God is leading us.

In Acts 13:2, the Holy Spirit spoke, and after fasting and prayer, the church at Antioch sent out Barnabas and Paul, who sailed to Cyprus. There Paul, filled with the Holy Spirit, told the sorcerer he encountered, named Elymas, that he was a child of the devil and an enemy of all that is right. He then declared that the sorcerer would be blind, and immediately Elymas could not see. The proconsul saw this and was amazed, and the Bible tells us that "he believed" (v. 12). In the days to come we will see these types of power encounters between followers of Jesus Christ and those who worship the "powers of this age, and the god of this age" or world.[6] Here's how I know.

In Matthew 24, the disciples asked Jesus what would be the sign of His coming and what would signal the end of the age. In verse 24, Jesus tells them that, among other end-time signals, false prophets and counterfeit messiahs would arise, and they would perform "great signs and wonders" intended to "deceive"—even God's own people, if they are not careful. *These* are what will point to the end of the age. Christ's coming will be preceded by an increase in fake signs and wonders—the types of "wonders" performed by today's practitioners of Reiki, healing touch, therapeutic touch, and so on. Many of these practitioners have spent a lifetime perfecting their "craft," but their power is not from God. Their "healings" are lying wonders.

And these are not the only signs and wonders that will be seen at the end of this age. There will also be "great signs"—performed by the beast that we read about in Revelation 13, whose miracles will cause earth's inhabitants to worship the Antichrist. Now, we know that this beast, and the evil power behind him, will be defeated and Christ will reign forever in His kingdom, but not before many are deceived, just before Christ's return.

So, the fact that there are so many more healings and miracles happening today, both within the church and through the powers of this evil age, should awaken us to the fact that we are living in the *last* of the last days. So how do we tell the difference between the truth and a lie, the genuine and the counterfeit?

Here are the safeguards for discernment: If those who are performing signs and wonders are pointing people to Jesus, and the miracles they perform result in the worship of Him, you need not fear that you are seeing a lying wonder. It is the power of God at work. But if something is done that does *not* acknowledge Jesus Christ, even though it may look like the same thing, ask yourself: "Is this evoking the worship of God? Does this person acknowledge the incarnation of Jesus?" If the answer to these questions is no, then the power of darkness is at work—and it is your job to confront it, just as the apostle Paul confronted Elymas in the book of Acts.

We are told that in the last days, God will pour out His Spirit on all people (Joel 2:28; Acts 2:17–18). We are also promised that signs will accompany those who believe. What signs? "They will place their hands on sick people, and they will get well" (Mark 16:18). Further, these "signs" will confirm the Word of God—that life-changing gospel that we are commissioned to preach to "all the world" (Mark 16:15).

May you believe and expect to see God's miraculous power at work in your life and in your church in this time—the end of the end times—when the earth is "filled with the knowledge of the glory of the LORD as the waters cover the sea" (Hab. 2:14). The "glory of the

Lord" is most revealed through His mighty power to work signs and wonders, healing and miracles, and He wants to work them through *you*. In the next chapter I will share how you can better cooperate with God as you, like the apostle Paul, "strenuously contend with all the energy Christ so powerfully works" in you (Col. 1:29).

CHAPTER 15

BEING USED BY GOD TO BRING HEALING

WHERE DO WE GO FROM HERE?

If by now you're convinced that miracles both happened in the past and still happen today, or you are at least open to the possibility, you may be asking, "So what's the next step? How can I experience more from God? And how can *I* be enabled to participate in the end-times revival?

I have dedicated nearly fifty years to ministry. For almost thirty-five of those years I have placed a high priority on equipping, especially normal believers—Christians—to experience, understand, and be used by God's Holy Spirit. I have taught hundreds of thousands of people on five continents in these matters. I hope to be equipping the saints until the day I leave this earth and transition into a greater, richer, more exciting existence with Christ.

Let me suggest several ways you can receive training, knowledge, understanding, and experience in being used by God's Spirit to bring healing to someone's body and/or soul. These are great opportunities that, if acted upon, will enable you to become more powerful, knowledgeable, and loving than you are presently.

First, read and study more of my books and avail yourself of the other resources I have prepared. The *Power to Heal Curriculum*[1] is a full program that contains my book *The Power to Heal*, a workbook, a leader's guide on DVD, and a DVD containing eight video teachings to go with the chapters in the book. Many pastors have been using this in their churches for small groups or Sunday school classes. You could gather friends together and turn your living room into a training center with friends and/or family. Everything you need to lead a training clinic in your home is provided in the kit.

Another curriculum I recommend is *The Essential Guide to Healing Curriculum*.[2] It is a twelve-week program that contains the book *The Essential Guide to Healing*, a workbook, a leader's guide, and a DVD with teachings that go along with the reading each week. One half of this curriculum was written by my friend Bill Johnson, and the other half by me.

A third curriculum is the *Authority to Heal Curriculum*.[3] It is similar to the first two, but it goes into more details that are not covered in the others. It is not the one to start with, but the one to finish with.

You can also sign up to take the online course, the *Christian Healing Certification Program*. This program can be viewed, with all its details, including the professors, three tracks, twelve courses, and how to become certified, at https://healingcertification.com. The three tracks are Physical Healing, Inner Healing, and Deliverance. Each track has four courses, and each course is eight weeks long.

This is not a glorified correspondence course. It is based on the best of online learning principles. You will be taking the course with up to fifteen others from all over the world, and a course facilitator will help you and your companions. A community is built among the group as you encourage one another and correspond by e-mail, Skype, and telephone. The physical healing portion of this course has been offered at Regent University Divinity School in Virginia. It is also offered at the United Methodist seminary, United Theological Seminary. Finally, this course is also available through the Global Awakening Theological Seminary. All of these are accredited by the US Department of Education, the highest and most important accreditation possible. Presently I am involved in teaching both courses with the aid of my assistant teacher, Dr. Robert Burge, who wrote his doctoral thesis on evaluating the success of the program.

You may not be as interested in healing as you are in prophecy and prophetic ministry. If so, the Christian Prophetic Certification Program is available. This program can be viewed with all of its five courses (each eight weeks long) at propheticcertification.com. It is structured the same way as the Christian Healing Certification Program. In just three years we have had more than 5,390 courses taken. That does not include the students at Regent Divinity School or United Theological Seminary and Global Awakening Theological Seminary. The course is the same, but you receive credit at the seminaries.

You can also attend one of our four-day schools, our Schools of Healing and Impartation. We have four different schools. One is called Foundations and is my favorite. There is a strong emphasis not just on learning about healing and hearing from God, but also on impartation. What is an impartation? It is when God comes upon you and empowers you or gifts you for moving in the gifts of the Holy Spirit. The three gifts we see most frequently activated are healing, words of knowledge, and prophecy. The second of these four-day events is called Empowered. It, too, focuses on healing, but also deals with deliverance. which is not usually addressed in the Foundations school. A third school, which is not often offered, is Healing: Spiritual and Medical Perspectives. The fourth school is Faith and Healing, which looks at the relationship between faith and healing. In this school you will study the faith cure movement of the nineteenth century and the Word of Faith movement and gain insight regarding faith's relationship to healing.

These schools occur all over the United States, usually one a month, except for April, July, and October, when we have our two largest conferences. We also have a training trip for thirteen- to twenty-nine-year-olds in Brazil.

All the above-mentioned schools involve four things: information, inspiration, activation, and impartation. Each four-day school is made up of twenty-four sessions. There are usually three to four speakers, and I typically teach half of the lectures.

Another opportunity for training and equipping is offered at our headquarters, by becoming a student in the Global School of Supernatural Ministry (Global School). Our nine-month, on-campus school offers both a one-year track and a two-year track, as well as internships with Global Awakening by invitation only for a possible third year. You can receive one to two years' worth of credits from an accredited Christian college for attending the on-campus school. There are also satellite schools where you can be part of a smaller student body closer to your home. And there is an online version of the school (it is only for the first year at this time). Many of our graduates have become missionaries, itinerate ministers, or pastors.

Which opportunity is for you? It depends on the amount of time, energy, and money you want to or can invest in your own personal spiritual development. What is best for you could be very different from someone else's needs. Our trained advisors will help you discover the best way for you. Contact our office for answers to what you should do next.

Bill Johnson, when asked how to advance in the things of the Spirit, gives people several suggestions, but he always ends by saying, "The fastest way to grow in moving in the gifts, and especially in words of knowledge and healing, is to go on an international ministry trip with Randy Clark and Global Awakening." We have had about five thousand people go with us to other nations, and almost 100 percent of them have seen someone healed when they prayed. Similarly, nearly 100 percent have had words of knowledge while on the trip. Global Awakening conducts about ten to twelve of these trips per year.

Finally, a little more detail about the Global Awakening Theological Seminary: My ministry partnered with another ministry and the Family of Faith University, an accredited Christian university. Together, we are now able to offer an accredited master of divinity degree, a three-year, seventy-two-hour program after your bachelor's degree. We are offering a master's in evangelism and a master's in pastoral ministry; these are two-year post-bachelor degrees. A four-year bachelor's degree is also available from the university.

If none of these options will work for you, I encourage you to go to our online bookstore. I have written about forty books, training manuals, and smaller booklets that are available there, along with many DVDs, CDs, and other products, including the three curricula mentioned earlier. Visit Globalawakeningstore.com.

Information about any of these other opportunities can be found on our Web page, Globalawakening.com. The times, costs, and all details are available there.

I want to encourage you to believe in God's ability and desire to use you to heal physical illnesses of others, to deliver the oppressed, to heal the brokenhearted, to bring back those who have walked away from God, to proclaim the good news of the gospel, and to see people experience the new birth by accepting Jesus—spiritual regeneration. In other words, believe we really are ambassadors of His kingdom in which there is reconciliation to God (2 Cor. 5:20).

Jesus invites us into the "greater" things (John 14:12). He invites us to become His colaborers in the building of His eternal kingdom (see Mark 1:17).

Let us remember that God gives the Spirit to us without measure (John 3:34). He offers the Holy Spirit freely to those who ask Him (Luke 11:13). Jesus died to initiate the new covenant, which is the pouring out of the Spirit into the hearts of God's people. He not only brings this new covenant into existence by His death, but He then becomes the Baptizer in the Spirit by His life (Mark 1:8; Rom. 5:12–20). One of His first resurrection acts was to meet His disciples, commission them, and blow upon them, telling them to receive the Holy Spirit. Then He told them that "as the Father has sent Me, I also send you" (John 20:21 NASB).

We must consider all this. The Father sent Jesus to the world being conceived of the Spirit. When we are born again, we, too, are born of the Spirit (John 3:6). Yet, Jesus did not begin His ministry until after He was baptized and filled with the Spirit (Matt. 3:16). It was only after this empowerment that Jesus did any mighty deeds or commenced His ministry. We are sent as the Father sent Jesus. Jesus realized the importance of this empowerment and told His disciples to wait in Jerusalem until they were clothed with power. When the Holy Spirit came upon them, He promised, they would receive that power (Luke 24:49; Acts 1:8).

For this grace to be released, the new covenant had to be enacted through His death and resurrected life. This grace wasn't only for the forgiveness of sins. It was also for the divine enablement of the followers of Jesus. It wasn't only to get us to heaven, but to bring the power of heaven to us. This is why it is to our advantage that Jesus was crucified, was raised, and ascended to the Father, so that we could have a divine enablement of power and authority to do what He did and greater things. Mark's Gospel ends with a great commission that includes our ability to lay our hands upon the sick and see them healed. This is one of the signs that is to accompany those who have believed (Mark 16:17–18). This grace to heal was not limited to the apostles, or to pastors or evangelists. No, it is available to *those who have believed*. Furthermore, biblical discipleship is to include the teaching of the new believers to obey the commandments of Jesus; at the top of the list of His commandments in the commissioning of the Twelve and of the seventy or seventy-two is to heal the sick and cast out demons.

Being a Christian was never meant to be boring. It is an invitation to an experience, a relationship, and power that is *out of this world*. It is an invitation into the supernatural, an opportunity to see miracles and regularly experience healings. It is an invitation to be, not only clothed with power, but also commissioned with authority to have access to the power and authority of Jesus' name. We are His ambassadors, backed up by His kingdom.

You have inherited so much more than you have appropriated, if you are in Christ. I challenge you to step out in His authority and experience His power. Step into the light and watch the darkness yield to it. This is God's plan for you—this is the new covenant privilege of an empowered life, not just an eternal life!

Oh, in case you think I am not in touch with reality and that I believe that all of life will be perfect if you follow Christ, let me assure you: I know better. And I want to encourage you who may have the misfortune of being faced with tragedy in your lives, perhaps the loss of loved ones or other major losses. For you, too, this miraculous power is important. You don't have to walk through the valley of the shadow of death in your own strength. You don't have to experience the dark nights of the soul alone. Jesus will be with you! He will place His shoulder in the double yoke and strengthen you to not falter under the weight of tragedy and disappointments. His power and His comfort, along with His peace, can enable us to live victoriously when life's tragedies strike. Those who see the difference in how we walk through these times will recognize there is a miraculous power at work in us. It enables us to be faithful to the end and not lose hope but to experience the One who promised to stick closer than a brother, who would never leave us or forsake us. He embraced such suffering at His cross, but He rose victoriously. So we can not only endure such times of life, when the sun seems to be hidden behind the clouds of problems, but we can experience His joy as we walk through them (Col. 1:11–12).

Let us end with the words of the apostle Paul: "But we have this treasure in jars of clay to show that this all-surpassing power is from God and not from us. We are hard pressed on every side, but not crushed; perplexed, but not in despair; persecuted, but not abandoned; struck down, but not destroyed" (2 Cor. 4:7–9). We are, in fact, "more than conquerors" through Christ! (Rom. 8:37).

NOTE FROM THE AUTHOR

I have received endorsements from seminary professors of theology—Old Testament and New Testament—seminary academic deans, endorsements from Anglicans, Roman Catholics, United Methodists, Baptists, Christian Missionary Alliance, and the Redeemed Christian Church of God in Nigeria (the world's largest church). Also, there have been endorsements from medical doctors, psychiatrists, and professors at medical schools; from professors of religion at state universities, as well as endorsements from general overseers, bishops, district superintendents, and overseers of new Apostolic networks. This indicates the diversity and wealth of expertise of those who have endorsed *Eyewitness to Miracles*. I have tried to write *Eyewitness to Miracles* for the entire church. I have not wanted to have a sectarian spirit. It is my desire, hope, and prayer, that millions of people will be encouraged by *Eyewitness to Miracles*, and that it will encourage you to believe the words of Jesus about the power of His rule and reign available to all who believe in Him in our day-to-day lives.

APPENDIX A

THE NEW TESTAMENT EVIDENCE

Following is a list of all the references to words pertaining to miracles or supernatural manifestations, or more biblically speaking, God's mighty acts, His deeds, the displays of His power, or situations where God's power is revealed even if none of the words associated with power are used. All scriptures on this list are from the New American Standard Bible.

"These signs will accompany those who have believed: in My name they will cast out demons, they will speak with new tongues." (Mark 16:17)

And they went out and preached everywhere, while the Lord worked with them, and confirmed the word by the signs that followed. (Mark 16:20)

"This will be a sign for you: you will find a baby wrapped in cloths and lying in a manger." (Luke 2:12)

And Simeon blessed them and said to Mary His mother, "Behold, this Child is appointed for the fall and rise of many in Israel, and for a sign to be opposed." (Luke 2:34)

This beginning of His signs Jesus did in Cana of Galilee, and manifested His glory, and His disciples believed in Him. (John 2:11)

Now when He was in Jerusalem at the Passover, during the feast, many believed in His name, observing His signs which He was doing. (John 2:23)

This man came to Jesus by night and said to Him, "Rabbi, we know that You have come from God as a teacher; for no one can do these signs that You do unless God is with him." (John 3:2)

This is again a second sign that Jesus performed when He had come out of Judea into Galilee. (John 4:54)

A large crowd followed Him, because they saw the signs which He was performing on those who were sick. (John 6:2)

Therefore when the people saw the sign which He had performed, they said, "This is truly the Prophet who is to come into the world." (John 6:14)

Jesus answered them and said, "Truly, truly, I say to you, you seek Me, not because you saw signs, but because you ate of the loaves and were filled. (John 6:26)

So they said to Him, "What then do You do for a sign, so that we may see, and believe You? What work do You perform? (John 6:30)

But many of the crowd believed in Him; and they were saying, "When the Christ comes, He will not perform more signs than those which this man has, will He?" (John 7:31)

Therefore the chief priests and the Pharisees convened a council, and were saying, "What are we doing? For this man is performing many signs." (John 11:47)

For this reason also the people went and met Him, because they heard that He had performed this sign. (John 12:18)

But though He had performed so many signs before them, yet they were not believing in Him. (John 12:37)

Therefore many other signs Jesus also performed in the presence of the disciples, which are not written in this book. (John 20:30)

"And I will grant wonders in the sky above and signs on the earth below, blood, and fire, and vapor of smoke." (Acts 2:19)

"Men of Israel, listen to these words: Jesus the Nazarene, a man attested to you by God with miracles and wonders and signs which God performed through Him in your midst, just as you yourselves know . . ." (Acts 2:22)

Everyone kept feeling a sense of awe; and many wonders and signs were taking place through the apostles. (Acts 2:43)

"What shall we do with these men? For the fact that a noteworthy miracle has taken place through them is apparent to all who live in Jerusalem, and we cannot deny it." (Acts 4:16)

". . . while You extend Your hand to heal, and signs and wonders take place through the name of Your holy servant Jesus." (Acts 4:30)

At the hands of the apostles many signs and wonders were taking place among the people; and they were all with one accord in Solomon's portico. (Acts 5:12)

And Stephen, full of grace and power, was performing great wonders and signs among the people. (Acts 6:8)

"This man led them out, performing wonders and signs in the land of Egypt and in the Red Sea and in the wilderness for forty years." (Acts 7:36)

The crowds with one accord were giving attention to what was said by Philip, as they heard and saw the signs which he was performing. (Acts 8:6)

Even Simon himself believed; and after being baptized, he continued on with Philip, and as he observed signs and great miracles taking place, he was constantly amazed. (Acts 8:13)

Therefore they spent a long time there speaking boldly with reliance upon the Lord, who was testifying to the word of His grace, granting that signs and wonders be done by their hands. (Acts 14:3)

All the people kept silent, and they were listening to Barnabas and Paul as they were relating what signs and wonders God had done through them among the Gentiles. (Acts 15:12)

". . . in the power of signs and wonders, in the power of the Spirit; so that from Jerusalem and round about as far as Illyricum I have fully preached the gospel of Christ." (Rom. 15:19)

The signs of a true apostle were performed among you with all perseverance, by signs and wonders and miracles. (2 Cor. 12:12)

God also testifying with them, both by signs and wonders and by various miracles and by gifts of the Holy Spirit according to His own will. (Heb. 2:4)

As you can see from these verses, the word *wonders* sometimes accompanies "signs"; in fact, all sixteen times the word *wonders* appears in the New Testament, it is paired with the word *signs*.

"For false Christs and false prophets will arise and will show great signs and wonders, so as to mislead, if possible, even the elect." (Matt. 24:24)

"For false Christs and false prophets will arise, and will show signs and wonders, in order to lead astray, if possible, the elect." (Mark 13:22)

So Jesus said to him, "Unless you people see signs and wonders, you simply will not believe." (John 4:48)

"And I will grant wonders in the sky above and signs on the earth below, blood, and fire, and vapor of smoke." (Acts 2:19)

". . . that is, the one whose coming is in accord with the activity of Satan, with all power and signs and false wonders . . ." (2 Thess. 2:9)

". . . God also testifying with them, both by signs and wonders and by various miracles and by gifts of the Holy Spirit according to His own will." (Heb. 2:4)

APPENDIX B

THE OLD TESTAMENT EVIDENCE

Signs and wonders don't just suddenly appear in the pages of our New Testament. We see *sign* used often, and along with wonders, in many Old Testament passages as well.

"But if they will not believe even these two signs or heed what you say, then you shall take some water from the Nile and pour it on the dry ground; and the water which you take from the Nile will become blood on the dry ground." (Ex. 4:9)

"You shall take in your hand this staff, with which you shall perform the signs." (Ex. 4:17)

Moses told Aaron all the words of the LORD with which He had sent him, and all the signs that He had commanded him to do. (Ex. 4:28)

And Aaron spoke all the words which the Lord had spoken to Moses. He then performed the signs in the sight of the people. (Ex. 4:30)

"But I will harden Pharaoh's heart that I may multiply My signs and My wonders in the land of Egypt." (Ex. 7:3)

"Or has a god tried to go to take for himself a nation from within another nation by trials, by signs and wonders and by war and by a mighty hand and by an outstretched arm and by great terrors, as the LORD your God did for you in Egypt before your eyes?" (Deut. 4:34)

"You shall bind them as a sign on your hand and they shall be as frontals on your forehead." (Deut. 6:8)

"Moreover, the LORD showed great and distressing signs and wonders before our eyes against Egypt, Pharaoh and all his household." (Deut. 6:22)

. . . the great trials which your eyes saw and the signs and the wonders and the mighty hand and the outstretched arm by which the LORD your God brought you out. So shall the LORD your God do to all the peoples of whom you are afraid. (Deut. 7:19)

. . . and His signs and His works which He did in the midst of Egypt to Pharaoh the king of Egypt and to all his land . . . (Deut. 11:3)

"You shall therefore impress these words of mine on your heart and on your soul; and you shall bind them as a sign on your hand, and they shall be as frontals on your forehead." (Deut. 11:18)

"If a prophet or a dreamer of dreams arises among you and gives you a sign or a wonder, and the sign or the wonder comes true, concerning which he spoke to you, saying, 'Let us go after other gods (whom you have not known) and let us serve them, . . .'" (Deut. 13:1–2)

"And the LORD brought us out of Egypt with a mighty hand and an outstretched arm and with great terror and with signs and wonders." (Deut. 26:8)

"They shall become a sign and a wonder on you and your descendants forever." (Deut. 28:46)

". . . the great trials which your eyes have seen, those great signs and wonders." (Deut. 29:3)

". . . for all the signs and wonders which the LORD sent him to perform in the land of Egypt against Pharaoh, all his servants, and all his land." (Deut. 34:11)

NOTES

Chapter 1: The Blind See

1. View this testimony using the playlist: https://globalawakening.com/eyewitnesstomiracles.

Chapter 2: The Lame Walk

1. View this testimony using the playlist: https://globalawakening.com/eyewitnesstomiracles.
2. View this testimony using the playlist: https://globalawakening.com/eyewitnesstomiracles.
3. *The New International Dictionary of Pentecostal and Charismatic Revised and Expanded Edition*, Stanley Burgess, editor and Edward M Van Der Mass associate editor, (Kindle locations 4–5).

Chapter 3: The Sick Are Healed

1. "Fall over" and "slumped to the floor" are references to a common phenomenon within the history of the church. It is caused by the strong presence of God, and has been referred to as losing all strength, swooning, falling under the power, slain in the Spirit, and resting in the Spirit. These are representative. This phenomenon is present in the Catholic, Protestant, and Pentecostal/Charismatic movements.
2. View this testimony using the playlist: https://globalawakening.com/eyewitnesstomiracles.
3. For more information on Rex and Lois Burgher, go to www.klifemin.org/ (Dillsburg, PA: Kingdom Life Ministry). Rex and Lois have written a book detailing their journey, *When the Fire Falls* (Dillsburg, PA: Kingdom Life Ministry, 2015), and Rex has written two other books, *Journey to Your*

Kingdom Destiny (Dillsburg, PA: Kingdom Life Ministry, 2013) and *Our Father's Heartbeat* (Dillsburg, PA: Kingdom Life Ministry, 2011).

4. View this testimony using the playlist: https://globalawakening.com/eyewitnesstomiracles.

5. View this testimony using the playlist: https://globalawakening.com/eyewitnesstomiracles.

6. Carole Baerg's story appears in Randy Clark, *There Is More! The Secret to Experiencing God's Power to Change Your Life* (Grand Rapids: Baker, 2013), 149–52.

Chapter 4: The Deaf Hear

1. See "Police Officer with Severed Spine Jumps out of Wheelchair," in chapter 2.

2. See Candy Gunther Brown, "Study of the Therapeutic Effects of Proximal Intercessory Prayer (STEPP) on Auditory and Visual Impairments in Rural Mozambique," *Southern Medical Journal* 103, no. 9 (September 2010); Candy Gunther Brown, *Testing Prayer: Science and Healing* (Cambridge, MA: Harvard University Press, 2012).

Chapter 5: The Dead Are Raised

1. Athet Pyan Shinthhaw Paulu, "The Remarkable Testimony of a Buddhist Monk in Myanmar (Burma) Who Came Back to Life a Changed Man!" BibleProbe.com, accessed November 2, 2017, http://www.bibleprobe.com/backfromthedead.htm.

2. James Rutz, *Mega Shift: Igniting Spiritual Power* (Colorado Springs: Empowerment Press, 2005), 34–35.

3. David Yonggi Cho, speaking at a church growth seminar in Salem Church (Helsinki, Finland, 1995).

4. From a conversation with Phillip Gammill, staff member with Freedom Ministries US Office (Raymondville, TX).

5. This is retold in Rutz, *Mega Shift*, 10–12, and confirmed in David Servant, "Pastor Daniel Ekechukwa and His Resurrection from the Dead: Report One of Four," the website of David Servant, accessed September 12, 2017, http://www.heavensfamily.org/ss/resurrection-from-the-dead-pastor-daniel-ekechukwu.

6. From a phone conversation with Phillip Gammill of Freedom Ministries Staff. Also reported in Rutz, *Mega Shift*, 13–14.

7. This story was taken from an interview on CBN. See CBN.com, "Dr. Chauncey Crandall: Raising the Dead," CBN, http://www1.cbn .com/content/dr-chauncey-crandall-raising-dead.

8. View this testimony using the playlist: https://globalawakening.com /eyewitnesstomiracles.

9. Ibid.

10. Ibid. This video is actually Surprise translating the dead-raising story of two dead babies being raised by Mrs. Donwecke, the wife of a regional overseer of Iris Ministries in Mozambique—she has raised four people from the dead, and her husband had raised three as of 2010. I do not know if there have been more raised by them since 2010.

Chapter 6: Religion and the Age of Enlightenment

1. Jon Ruthven, *What's Wrong with Protestant Theology: Tradition vs. Biblical Emphasis* (Tulsa: Word & Spirit Press, 2013), 110. Quoting the Harris Poll # 11, February 26, 2003; Harris Poll #90, December 14, 2005; HCD Research and the Louis Frankelstein Institute for Religious and Social Studies of the Jewish Theological Seminary in New York, December 23, 2004. http://www.wnd.com/index .php?pageId=28152; and the Ynet–Gesher poll was conducted by the Panels Research Institute and included five hundred respondents that constitute a representative sample of Jewish population in Israel. It was published December 23, 2008, in YNet News, http:www .ynetnewscom/articles/0,7340L-3642955,00.html (no longer accessible).

2. Luther prayed for both Melancthon and Myconius, fellow Reformers, and they were healed. Same for the other Reformers; there were reports of healings among Anabaptists.

3. Ruthven, *What's Wrong with Protestant Theology? Tradition vs. Biblical Emphasis* (Tulsa: Word & Spirit Press, 2013), 90; Jon Ruthven, *On the Cessation of the Charismata: The Protestant Polemic on Postbiblical Miracles* (Tulsa: Word & Spirit Press, 2011), 24.

Chapter 7: Science and the Laws of Nature

1. Voltaire, *The Works of Voltaire*, vol. 4 (Philosophical Dictionary Part 2)
   [1764], http://oll.libertyfund.org/titles/353#Voltaire_0060–04_1207;
   http://oll.libertyfund.org/titles/voltaire-the-works-of-voltaire-vol-iv
   -philosophical-dictionary-part-2. *Voltaire, The Works of Voltaire.*
   A Contemporary Version. A Critique and Biography by John Morley,
   notes by Tobias Smollett, trans. William F. Fleming (New York: E.R.
   DuMont, 1901), vol. 4 of 21, http://oll.libertyfund.org/titles/353#
   Voltaire_0060–04_1207.
2. The following biographical sketches are based on "Famous Scientists
   Who Believed in God," *Evidence for God*, accessed September 13, 2017,
   http://www.godandscience.org/apologetics/sciencefaith.html.
3. Francis Bacon, *Of Atheism*, repr. (n.p.: Kessinger, 2010).
4. See Rich Deem, "The Trinity: The Oneness and Plurality of God,"
   Evidence for God, accessed September 12, 2017, http://www.godand
   science.org/doctrine/trinity.html.
5. J. P. Moreland, *Love Your God with All Your Mind: The Role of Reason
   in the Life of the Soul* (Washington, DC: NavPress, 1997).
6. Rich Deem, "What Is Wrong with Pascal's Wager?" *Evidence for God*,
   accessed September 13, 2017, http://www.godandscience.org/apologetics
   /pascals_wager.html.
7. See Casey Luskin, "A Tall Tale of Evolution: The Neck of the Giraffe,"
   Evolution News, May 10, 2007, https://evolutionnews.org/2007/05/a_
   tall_tale_of_evolution_the_n/.
8. Fred Hoyle and Chandra Wickramasinghe, *Evolution from Space*
   (New York: Simon & Schuster, 1982), 27–28.

Chapter 8: Philosophy and Theology

1. Keener points out the circular argument in this Humean argument
   against the supernatural. Keener, *Miracles*, 1:85–106.
2. The following material is drawn from William De Arteaga, *Forging a
   Renewed Hebraic and Pauline Christianity* (Tulsa: Word & Spirit Press,
   forthcoming), 67n210. See the classic work by Christian historian Peter
   Gay, *The Enlightenment: An Interpretation*, vol. 1, *The Rise of Modern
   Paganism* (New York: Knopf, 1966), for an understanding of the

central role that anti-Christianity has in later Enlightenment thought. For a detailed study of this radical anti-Christian and atheistic core of the later Enlightenment, see Philipp Blom, *A Wicked Company: The Forgotten Radicalism of the European Enlightenment* (New York; Basic Books, 2010).

3. Ruthven, *On the Cessation of the Charismata*, 23 fn. 54.

4. Ruthven, *On the Cessation of the Charismata*, 24.

5. For more understanding see John Ruthven, *On the Cessation of the Charismata*.

6. Ruthven, *On the Cessation of the Charismata*, 26–27.

Chapter 9: Explaining Away the Miraculous

1. See "Late June and Early July Floods of 2002: Over The Texas Hill Country and South Central Texas," Weather.gov, accessed November 2, 2017, https://www.weather.gov/media/ewx/wxevents/ewx-2002 07.pdf.

2. Alastair H. B. Logan, "Marcellus of Ancyra and Anti-Arian Polemic," in *Studia Patristica*, ed. Elizabeth A. Livingstone (Leuven, BE: Peeters Press, 1989), 22:189, paraphrased.

3. Ruthven, *What's Wrong with Protestant Theology?*, 10–27, esp. 21n48; 83n81.

4. Robert Culpepper, *Evaluating the Charismatic Movement: A Theological and Biblical Appraisal* (King of Prussia, PA: Judson Press, 1977).

5. Archbishop Welby shared this with me in a meeting at his home with a few of my friends in 2015.

Chapter 10: Recovering the Ministry of Healing

1. Rudolf Bultmann, "A Reply to the Thesis of J. Schniewind," in *Kerygma and Myth: A Theological Debate*, ed. Hans Werner Bartach, trans. R. H. Fuller (London: SPCK, 1957).

2. Paul Chappell, *Dictionary of Pentecostal and Charismatic Movements*, ed. Stanley M. Burgess and Gary B. McGee (Grand Rapids: Zondervan, 1996), s.v. "Healing Movements," 353–74. For more insight into the faith cure movement, see Joe McIntyre, *E. W. Kenyon and His Message of Faith* (Bothell, WA: Empowering Grace, 2010); and Paul King,

Only Believe: Examining the Origin and Development of Classic and Contemporary "Word of Faith" Theologies (Tulsa: Word & Spirit, 2008).

3. Craig Keener, *Miracles* (Grand Rapids: Baker Academic, 2011).

4. Jack Deere, *Surprised by the Voice of God: How God Speaks Today Through Prophecies, Dreams, and Visions* (Grand Rapids: Zondervan, 1998), 53–54.

5. "From Toronto Blessing to Global Awakening: Healing and the Spread of Charismatic Networks," in Candy Gunther Brown, *Testing Prayer: Science and Healing* (Cambridge, MA: Harvard University Press, 2012), 21–63; Candy Brown, "Global Awakenings: Divine Healing Networks and Global Community in North America, Brazil, Mozambique, and Beyond," in Candy Gunther Brown, *Global Pentecostal and Charismatic Healing* (New York: Oxford University Press, 2011), 351–71.

Chapter 11: Verifying Healing

1. Randy Clark, "A Study of the Effects of Christian Prayer on Pain or Mobility Restrictions from Surgery Involving Implanted Materials" (DMin diss, United Theological Seminar, 2013).

2. Clark, v.

3. Clark, v.

4. R. Chou and L. H. Huffman, "American Pain Society, American College of Physicians: Nonpharmacologic Therapies for Acute and Chronic Low Back Pain: A Review of the Evidence for an American Pain Society/American College of Physicians Clinical Practice Guideline," *Annals of Internal Medicine* 147, no. 7 (2007): 492–504.

Chapter 12: Healing and the Placebo Effect

1. A. Hróbjartsson and P. C. Gøtzsche, "Is the Placebo Powerless? Update of a Systematic Review with 52 New Randomized Trials Comparing Placebo with No Treatment," *Journal of Internal Medicine-Oxford* 256, no. 2 (August 2004): 91–100. This article was based on research from the Cochrane Review Centre, Rigshospitalet, Copenhagen, Denmark. Donald D. Price, Damien G. Finniss, and Fabrizio Benedetti, "A Comprehensive Review of the Placebo Effect: Recent Advances and

Current Thought," *Annual Review of Psychology* 59 (January 2008): 565–90, http://www.annualreviews.org/doi/abs/10.1146/annurev.psych .59.113006.095941; Steven Novella, "The Placebo Effect," *Science-Based Medicine*, January 16, 2008, http://sciencebasedmedicine.org /the-placebo-effect/.

2. Herbert Benson, *Timeless Healing: The Power and Biology of Belief* (New York: Simon and Schuster, 1997), 166.

3. Chou and Huffman, "American Pain Society," 28 (see chap. 11, n. 4).

4. A. Hróbjartsson and P. C. Gøtzsche, "Is the Placebo Powerless?

5. Benson, *Timeless Healing,* 166, emphasis added.

6. Benson, 27.

7. Benson, 183.

8. Benson, 187, emphasis added.

9. Benson, 188.

10. Benson, 27. Benson believes that remembered wellness requires an expectation of healing.

11. "If you are pleased with me, *teach me your ways so I may know you and continue to find favor with you.* Remember that this nation is your people" (Ex. 33:13, emphasis added). Discovering the ways of God is related to knowing Him better, and is key to finding favor with God. To say it another way, the ministry of healing is much more successful when we stop focusing on trying to get God to bless what we are doing, and instead, we realize what He is doing, and bless what He is doing! This is based on revelation from God out of intimacy with God. It is rooted in the operation of His gifts, which are "gracelets" of His divine energy. For a thorough teaching on the ways of God, and the relationship between revelatory words like words of knowledge and their creating faith which releases the gifts of healing or working of miracles see my book, *Healing Breakthrough,* especially the last half of the book.

Chapter 13: Energy and a Case for Miracles

1. National Center for Complementary and Alternative Medicine (NCCAM), "More Than One-Third of U.S. Adults Use Complementary and Alternative Medicine, According to New Government Survey," May 27, 2004, http://nccam.nih.gov/news/2004/052704.htm.

2. Wouter J. Hanegraaff, *New Age Religion and Western Culture: Esotericism in the Mirror of Secular Thought* (Albany: State University of New York Press, 1988), 128–52, esp. 128, 143.

3. "The Spirit himself testifies with our spirit that we are God's children" (Rom. 8:16).

4. John P. Newport, *The New Age Movement and the Biblical Worldview: Conflict and Dialogue* (Grand Rapids: Eerdmans, 1998), 4–5.

5. I am aware that this term is a quote from Paul Tillich, a neo-orthodox or liberal theologian of the twentieth century. This term is used in Tillich's book, *The Courage to Be* (New Haven, CT: Yale University Press, 1952), 156–57. Tillich had pantheistic leanings, as the description of the "ground of being" in *The Courage to Be*, 186, demonstrates. Tillich was considered by some theologians to be a pantheist. (My systematic theology teacher in seminary, Dr. Dale Moody, had been Tillich's fellow at Union Theological Seminary in New York. He shared this pantheistic opinion of Tillich in class.) It is not my intention to connect Tillich to New Age or shamanism, but the term was helpful in trying to explain pantheism.

6. Gareth Leyshon, "A Catholic Critique of the Healing Art of Reiki," http://www.drgareth.info/Reiki_GL.pdf, accessed September 14, 2017; Gareth Leyshon, "Framing a Christian Response to New Age Practices: Core Issues and Pastoral Solutions," August 3, 2004, http://www .drgareth.info/NewAgeRP.pdf,; Committee on Doctrine, United States Conference of Catholic Bishops, "Guidelines for Evaluating Reiki as an Alternative Therapy," March 25, 2009, http://www.usccb.org/about /doctrine/publications/upload/evaluation-guidelines-finaltext-2009–03 .pdf. For an analysis of the New Age energy modalities of healing, see Pontifical Council for Culture, *Jesus Christ the Bearer of the Water of Life: A Christian Reflection on the "New Age,"* http://www.vatican.va /roman_curia/pontifical_councils/interelg/documents/rc_pc_interelg _doc_20030203_new-age_en.html; Gary S. Greig and Kevin N. Springer, eds., *The Kingdom and the Power: Are Healing and the Spiritual Gifts Used by Jesus and the Early Church Meant for the Church Today?* (Ventura, CA: Regal Books, 1993), 62, 179–88, 359–92, 413–20.

7. Concerning the tension between the kingdom of heaven and the powers of darkness, Peter Davis states that "in no area are the effects of sin

completely reversed in this age, although in all areas some reversal of each of the effects of sin occurs. Some tension always remains, even if there is a significant taste of 'the powers of the age to come' (Heb. 6:5).'" Peter H. Davis, "A Biblical View of the Relationship of Sin and the Fruit of Sin: Sickness, Demonization, Death, Natural Calamity," in Greig and Springer, *The Kingdom and the Power*, 126.

8. Rev. 11:15.

9. "Now the Lord is the Spirit, and where the Spirit of the Lord is, there is liberty. But we all, with unveiled face, beholding as in a mirror the glory of the Lord, are being transformed into the same image from glory to glory, just as from the Lord, the Spirit" (2 Cor. 3:17–18 NASB).

10. This is where I disagree with the too-limited understanding of the powers, held by Walter Wink. He limits them to social structures rather than disembodied spiritual personalities. I agree they can wreak havoc on society by influencing the social structures, but I also believe they can influence individuals. There is a need to address the issue of demonic influence in social structures and in human beings. It is not a choice between one or the other, but a both/and situation. Walter Wink, *The Powers That Be: Theology for a New Millennium* (Minneapolis: Augsburg Fortress Press, 1998), 1–5.

11. "The Trinity dwells in us by means of that in itself which is communicable—that is to say, by the energies which are common to the three hypostases [Father, Son, Spirit], or, in other words, by grace—for it is by this name that we know the deifying energies which, the Holy Spirit communicates to us. He who has the Spirit, who confers the gift, has at the same time the Son, through whom every gift is transmitted to us; he also has the Father, from whom comes every perfect gift. *In receiving the gift—the deifying energies—one receives at the same time the indwelling of the Holy Trinity*." Vladimir Lossky, *The Mystical Theology of the Eastern Church* (Yonkers, NY: Saint Vladimir Seminary Press, 1997), 86–87; emphasis added.

12. Ruth Mayeux Allen, *Pneumatology: The Spirit of Reiki* (Sewanee, TN: School of Theology of the University of the South, 2009); Ruth Mayeux Allen, *The Holy Spirit and the Spirit of Reiki: One Source, One Spirit: Interconnecting Theology, Science, and the Practice of Reiki* (Monteagle, TN: North Bluff, 2011).

13. 1 John 2:18, 22; 4:3.

14. John McDowell, "Barth's Nein to Emil Brunner," http://convencion bautista.com/yahoo_site_admin/assets/docs/Barth_Nein_to_ Brunner.23191706.pdf, accessed November 2, 2017; Clark Pinnock, "Karl Barth and Christian Apologetics," *Themelios* 2 (1977): 66–71; John W. Hart, *Karl Barth vs. Emil Brunner: The Formation and Dissolution of a Theological Alliance, 1916–1936* (New York: Peter Lang, 2001), 212–14; Gregg Strawbridge, "Karl Barth's Rejection of Natural Theology or an Exegesis of Romans 1:19–20," paper presented at the 1997 Evangelical Theological Society Meeting in San Francisco, http://www.wordmp3.com/files/gs/barth.htm, accessed September 14, 2017.

15. Leslie D. Weatherhead, *Psychology, Religion, and Healing* (Nashville: Abingdon, 1952); Leslie D. Weatherhead, *Wounded Spirits* (Nashville: Abingdon, 1962).

16. Donal O'Mathuna and Walt Larimore, *Alternative Medicine: The Options, the Claims, the Evidence, How to Choose Wisely* (Grand Rapids: Zondervan, 2007), 253, 255, 262.

17. The following works offer more insights into the discrepancy between theistic and pantheistic writers concerning the angelic realm or the view that all spiritual energy is the same without distinguishing that some is from God and some is from the kingdom of darkness: Weatherhead, *Psychology, Religion, and Healing*; Weatherhead, *Wounded Spirits* (theistic); Dora Kunz, *Spiritual Healing* (Wheaton, IL: Theosphical Publishing House, 2009) (pantheistic). For more information on the issue of angels, demons, healing, and discernment and how they relate to one another, see Daniel Benor, *Spiritual Healing: Scientific Validation of a Healing Revolution* (Southfield, MI: Vision, 2001) (pantheistic, New Age); Gregory Boyd, *God at War: The Bible and Spiritual Conflict* (Downers Grove, IL: InterVarsity Press, 1997) (theistic); Randy Clark, *Open Heaven: Engaging the Unseen Realm* (Mechanicsburg, PA: Apostolic Network of Global Awakening, 2011) (theistic); Randy Clark, *School of Healing and Impartation: Deliverance, Disbelief, and Deception Workbook*, 3rd ed. (Mechanicsburg, PA: Global Awakening, 2009) (theistic); O'Mathuna

and Larimore, *Alternative Medicine* (theistic); Hanegraaff, *New Age Religion and Western Culture* (theistic); George Otis Jr., *The Twilight Labyrinth: Why Does Spiritual Darkness Linger Where It Does?* (Grand Rapids: Chosen Books, 1997) (theistic); Rhonda J. McClinton, *Spirits of the Lesser Gods: A Critical Examination of Reiki and Christ-Centered Healing* (Boca Raton, FL: Dissertation.com, 2007) (theistic); Erwin Van Der Meer, "The Strategic Level Spiritual Warfare Theology of C. Peter Wagner and Its Implications for Christian Mission in Malawi" (ThD thesis, University of South Africa, 2008), http://uir .unisa.ac.za/handle/10500/2891 (theistic); Michael S. B. Reid, *Strategic Level Spiritual Warfare: A Modern Mythology? A Detailed Evaluation of the Biblical, Theological and Historical Basis of Spiritual Warfare in Contemporary Thought* (Brentwood, Essex: Michael Reid Ministries, 2002) (theistic); Michael Donald Richardson, "Lessons from the Revival in Argentina" (DMin thesis, Fuller Theological Seminary, 1998) (theistic), https://www.researchgate.net/publication/36244700_ Lessons_from_the_revival_in_Argentina; Rev. Omar Cabrera Sr. and Omar Cabrera Jr., interview with author, trans. Rev. Henry Clay, Buenos Aires, June 16, 1996 (theistic); International Center for Reiki Training, "What Is Reiki?" http://www.reiki.org/faq/whatisreiki .html, accessed September 14, 2017 (pantheistic); Therapeutic Touch Organization, "Therapeutic Touch Home Page at Pumpkin Hollow Farm—The Northeast Theosophical Retreat Center," http://www .pumpkinhollow.org/content/therapeutic-touch-and-pumpkin-hollow; C. Peter Wagner, *Spiritual Warfare Strategies: Confronting Spiritual Powers* (Shippensburg, PA: Destiny Image, 1996) (theistic); C. Peter Wagner, *Territorial Spirits: Practical Strategies for How to Crush the Enemy through Spiritual Warfare* (Shippensburg, PA: Destiny Image, 2012) (theistic); Friedrich Zuendel, *The Awakening: One Man's Battle with Darkness* (n.p.: Plough, 1999) (theistic).

18. Finney feared for his life due to this power. Charles G. Finney, *An Autobiography* (Old Tappan, NJ: Fleming H. Revell, 1876), 20–21. D. L. Moody expressed concern that he would die if the power continued over his body; R. A. Torrey, "Why God Used D. L. Moody," in *The D. L. Moody Collections*, ed. James S. Bell (Chicago: Moody

Press, 1997), 116–17. Heidi Baker expressed the same concern that the power was enough to kill her. Randy Clark, *There Is More: The Secret to Experiencing God's Power to Change Your Life* (Grand Rapids: Baker, 2013), 66. I had the same experience. Randy Clark, *Baptism in the Holy Spirit* (Mechanicsburg, PA: Global Awakening, 2006), 37–43.

19. Billy Graham, *The Holy Spirit: Activating God's Power in Your Life* (Nashville: Thomas Nelson, 2000), 5.

20. Perhaps this was the position of Weatherhead regarding Odic force, as he made a distinction between divine healing and healing by Odic force. Weatherhead, *Wounded Spirits*, 49–65, with a definition of Odic force on 53.

21. "But we all, with unveiled face, beholding as in a mirror the glory of the Lord, are being transformed into the same image from glory to glory, just as from the Lord, the Spirit" (2 Cor. 3:18 NASB).

22. "Are not all angels *ministering* spirits sent to serve those who will inherit salvation?" (Heb. 1:14; emphasis added).

23. "He had a dream in which he saw a stairway resting on the earth, with its top reaching to heaven, and the angels of God were *ascending* and descending on it" (Gen. 28:12, emphasis added). "He then added, 'Very truly I tell you, you will see 'heaven open, and the angels of God *ascending and descending* on' the Son of Man'" (John 1:51, emphasis added).

24. Dora Kunz and Dolores Krieger, *The Spiritual Dimension of Therapeutic Touch* (Rochester, VT: Bear, 2004), 225–29.

25. Committee on Doctrine, United States Conference of Catholic Bishops, "Guidelines for Evaluating Reiki as an Alternative Therapy," 6n9.

26. Kunz and Krieger, *The Spiritual Dimension of Therapeutic Touch*, 225–29.

27. The message of grace in Jesus moves the focus from a *karmic* worldview to the gospel of not only undeserved forgiveness, but also undeserved healing—it is the gospel. See the distinction Bono of U2 made between grace and karma, in "Bono: Grace over Karma," August 1, 2005, *Christianity Today*, http://www.christianitytoday .com/ct/2005/augustweb-only/bono-0805.html; Jon Kuhrt, "Bono on the Difference Between Grace and Karma," *Resistance & Renewal* (blog), January 26, 2014, https://resistanceandrenewal.net/2014/01/26 /bono-on-the-difference-between-grace-and-karma/; "Bono Talking

About Grace," YouTube video, 4:07, posted by "2009zooropa,"
December 17, 2011, https://www.youtube.com/watch?v=nNE6GO
ClvrU. There are many other Internet links to Bono and his religious
views, especially regarding grace.

28. "And Jesus answering, saith to them: Have the faith of God. Amen I
say to you, that whosoever shall say to this mountain, Be thou removed
and be cast into the sea, and shall not stagger in his heart, but believe,
that whatsoever he saith shall be done; it shall be done unto him"
(Mark 11:22–23 DRA). The Douay-Rheims translation of 1 Cor. 13:2
is: "And if I should have all faith, so that I could remove mountains,
and have not charity, I am nothing." Mark 11:22 has "faith of God"
instead of "faith in God" in a recent Russian and German translation.
The new *Passion Bible* translates Mark 11:22 as *faith of God* rather than
faith in God.

29. Walter Wink, *The Powers That Be: Theology for a New Millennium*
(New York: Doubleday, 1998). This book brings together insights from
three of his earlier books, *Naming the Powers* (Minneapolis: Fortress
Press, 1984); *Unmasking the Powers* (Minneapolis: Fortress Press,
1986); and *Engaging the Powers* (Minneapolis: Augsburg Press, 1992).
This is not a small side issue. The amount of sickness, disease, and
poverty that is related to the effects of war is significant. Ministries
of healing must try to bring healing to the roots of the problem, not
merely the fruit of the problem. As wonderful and insightful as Wink's
works are, their weakness is their denying the reality of the lowly
personal demon in the life of a human. This is not an either-or choice
between the traditional conservative view of the personal demonic and
Wink's understanding of structural evil as demonic; it can be a both/
and choice.

30. Dora Kunz, *Spiritual Healing*, repr. (Canadian Theosophical
Association, January 28, 2009), http://www.theosophical.ca/books/
SpiritualHealing_DoraKunz.pdf, 2. This was originally a talk given in
Indralaya on July 30, 1957. It was transcribed and sent to Kunz's circle
of influence.

31. Kunz, 3.

32. Kunz, 2.

Chapter 14: Mount Carmel and the Coming End- Times Revival

1. Walter Wink, *The Powers That Be: Theology for a New Millennium*

2. For more explanation and defense for this understanding of faith see Jon Ruthven, *What's Wrong with Protestant Theology? Tradition vs. Biblical Emphasis* (Tulsa: Word & Spirit Press, 2013).

3. Psalms 105:37 KJV; some translations say *no one stumbled*.

4. This prophecy was well known among the Vineyard movement, of which I was a part for sixteen years. I believe it was known outside the movement as well.

5. John Wimber, *Power Evangelism* (Grand Rapids: Chosen Books, 1986, 2009); *Power Healing* (San Francisco: Harper and Row, 1987).

6. 2 Corinthians 4:4 (NIV, *age* /ESV-*world*).

Chapter 15: Being Used by God to Bring Healing

1. *Power to Heal Curriculum: 8 Weeks to Activating God's Healing Power in Your Life* (Destiny Image, 2015). Also, available through our website: http:// www.globalawakeningstore.com.

2. *The Kit: Equipping All Christians to Pray for the Sick* (Chosen Books, 2016).

3. *Authority to Heal Curriculum: Restoring the Lost Inheritance of God's Healing Power* (Destiny Image, 2017). Also, available through our website. www.globalawakeningstore.com.

BIBLIOGRAPHY

Allen, Ruth. *Pneumatology: The Spirit of Reiki*. Sewanee, TN: School of Theology of the University of the South, 2009.

———. *The Holy Spirit and the Spirit of Reiki: One Source, One Spirit: Interconnecting Theology, Science, and the Practice of Reiki*. Monteagle, TN: North Bluff, 2011.

Benor, Daniel. *Spiritual Healing: Scientific Validation of a Healing Revolution*. Southfield, MI: Vision, 2001.

Benson, Herbert. *Timeless Healing: The Power and Biology of Belief*. New York, NY: Simon & Schuster, 1997.

Boyd, Gregory. *God at War: The Bible and Spiritual Conflict*. Downers Grove, IL: InterVarsity Press, 1997.

Brown, Candy. "Study of the Therapeutic Effects of Proximal Intercessory Prayer (STEPP) on Auditory and Visual Impairments in Rural Mozambique." *Southern Medical Journal* 103, no. 9 (September 2010).

———. *Testing Prayer: Science and Healing*. Cambridge, MA: Harvard Univ. Press, 2012.

Bultmann, Rudolf. "A Reply to the Thesis of J. Schniewind." In *Kerygma and Myth: A Theological Debate*. London, UK: SPCK, 1957.

Chappell, Paul. *Dictionary of Pentecostal and Charismatic Movements*. Grand Rapids, MI: Zondervan, 1996.

Chou, R., and L. H. Huffman. "American Pain Society, American College of Physicians: Non-Pharmacologic Therapies for Acute and Chronic Low Back Pain: A Review of the Evidence for an American

Pain Society/American College of Physicians Clinical Practice Guideline." *Annual of Internal Medicine* 147, no. 7 (2007).

Clark, Randy. "A Study of the Effects of Christian Prayer on Pain or Mobility Restrictions from Surgery Involving Implanted Materials." Doctor of Ministry, United Theological Seminary, 2013.

———. *Open Heaven: Engaging the Unseen Realm.* Mechanicsburg, PA: Apostolic Network of Global Awakening, 2011.

———. *School of Healing and Impartation: Deliverance, Disbelief, and Deception Workbook.* 3rd ed. Mechanicsburg, PA: Global Awakening, 2009.

———. *There Is More! The Secret to Experiencing God's Power to Change Your Life.* Grand Rapids, MI: Baker, 2013.

Clark, Randy, Timothy Berry, Annie Byrne, and Chris Ishak. *Entertaining Angels: Engaging the Unseen Realm.* Mechanicsburg, PA: Apostolic Network of Global Awakening, 2008.

Cruz, Joan. *Mysteries, Marvels, Miracles: In the Lives of the Saints.* Rockville, IL: TAN Books, 1997.

Culpepper, Robert. *Evaluating the Charismatic Movement.* King of Prussia, PA: Judson Press, 1977.

DeArteaga. *Forging a Renewed Hebraic and Pauline Christianity.* Tulsa, OK: Word & Spirit Press, Forthcoming.

Deem, Richard. "Famous Scientists Who Believed in God," 2011. http://www.godandscience.org/apologetics/sciencefaith.html.

"Dr. Chauncey Crandall: A Patient Raised from the Dead." Christian Broadcast Network, n.d. http://www1.cbn.com/content/dr-chauncey-crandall-patient-raised-dead.

Fee, Gordon. *New Testament Series, Vols. 1–18.* New International Commentary on the New Testament. Grand Rapids, MI: Eerdmans, 2012.

Finney, Charles. *An Autobiography.* Old Tappan, NJ: Fleming H. Revell, 1876.

Fudge, Edward. *The Fire That Consumes: A Biblical and Historical Study of the Doctrine of Final Punishment.* Eugene, OR: Wipf & Stock, 2011.

Fudge, Edward, and Robert Peterson. *Two Views of Hell: A Biblical and Theological Dialogue.* Downers Grove, IL: IVP Academic, 2000.

Graham, Billy. *The Holy Spirit: Activating God's Power in Your Life.* Nashville, TN: Thomas Nelson, 2000.

Greig, Gary, and Kevin Springer. *The Kingdom and the Power: Are Healing and the Spiritual Gifts Used by Jesus and the Early Church Meant for the Church Today?* Ventura, CA: Regal Books, 1993.

Hanegraaff, Wouter. *New Age Religion and Western Culture: Esotericism in the Mirror of Secular Thought.* Albany, NY: State University of New York Press, 1988.

Hart, John. *Karl Barth vs. Emil Brunner: The Formation and Dissolution of a Theological Alliance, 1916–1936.* New York, NY: Peter Lang, 2001.

Hoyle, Fred, and Chandra Wickramasinge. *Evolution from Space.* New York, NY: Simon & Schuster, 1982.

Hrobjartsson, A., and P. C. Gøtzsche. "Is the Placebo Powerless? Update of a Systematic Review with 52 New Randomized Trials Comparing Placebo with No Treatment." *Journal of Internal Medicine* 256, no. 2 (August 2004): 91–100.

Jackson, John. John Paul Jackson Testimony, n.d. https://s3.amazonaws. com/GA-Podcast/testimonyPodcast/Episode11_John_Paul_Jackson_ Testimony.mp4.

Keener, Craig. *Miracles.* Grand Rapids, MI: Baker Academic, 2011.

King, Paul. *Only Believe: Examining the Origin and Development of Classic and Contemporary "Word of Faith" Theologies.* Tulsa, OK: Word & Spirit Press, 2008.

Kunz, Dora. *Spiritual Healing.* Wheaton, IL: Theosophical Pub. House, 2009. www.theosophical.ca/books/SpiritualHealing_DoraKunz.pdf.

———. *The Spiritual Dimension of Therapeutic Touch.* Rochester, VT: Bear, 2004.

Leyshon, Gareth. "A Catholic Critique of the Healing Art of Reiki," n.d. http://www.drgareth.info/Reiki_GL.pdf.

———. "Framing a Christian Response to New Age Practices: Core Issues and Pastoral Solutions," n.d. http://www.drgareth.info/NewAgeRP.pdf.

Logan, Alastair. "Marcellus of Ancyra and Anti-Arian Polemic." *Studia Patristica* 21 (1989).

Lossky, Vladimir. *The Mystical Theology of the Eastern Church.* Yonkers, NY: Saint Vladimir Seminary Press, 1997.

Louw, J. P., and E. A. Nida. *Greek-English Lexicon of the New Testament: Based on Semantic Domains.* New York, NY: United Bible Societies, 1996.

MacNutt, Judith. *Angels Are for Real: Inspiring, True Stories and Biblical Answers.* Grand Rapids, MI: Baker, 2012.

McClinton, Rhonda. "Spirits of the Lesser Gods: A Critical Examination of Reiki and Christ-Centered Healing." n.d. Dissertation.com.

McDowell, John. "Barth's Nein to Emil Brunner," n.d. http://www .freewebs.com/johnmcdowell/Lectures/THEO3002%20%282012 %29/Lecture%20-%20Barth%20vs%20Brunner.pdf.

McIntyre, Joe. *E. W. Kenyon and His Message of Faith.* Bothell, WA: Empowering Grace, 2010.

McKie, Robin. "Fred Hoyle: The Scientist Whose Rudeness Cost Him a Nobel Prize." *Guardian.* October 2, 2010.

Moody, Raymond. *Life After Life: The Investigation of a Phenomenon— Survival of Bodily Death.* Atlanta, GA: Mockingbird Books, 1975.

"More Than One-Third of U.S. Adults Use Complementary and Alternative Medicine, According to New Government Survey." National Center for Complementary and Alternative Medicine, 2004. http://nccam.nih.gov/news/2004/052704.htm.

Moreland, J. P. *Love Your God with All Your Mind: The Role of Reason in the Life of the Soul.* Washington, D.C.: NavPress, 1997.

Newport, John. *The New Age Movement and the Biblical Worldview: Conflict and Dialogue.* Grand Rapids, MI: Eerdmans, 1998.

Oates, Gary. *Open My Eyes, Lord: A Practical Guide to Angelic Visitations and Heavenly Experiences.* Open Heaven Publications, 2005.

O'Mathuna, Donald, and Walt Larimore. *Alternative Medicine: The Options, the Claims, the Evidence, How to Choose Wisely.* Grand Rapids, MI: Zondervan, 2007.

Otis, George. *The Twilight Labyrinth: Why Does Spiritual Darkness Linger Where It Does?* Grand Rapids, MI: Chosen Books, 1997.

Paulu, Athet Pyan Shinthaw. "The Remarkable Testimony of a Buddhist Monk in Myanmar (Burma) Who Came back to Life a Changed Man!" BibleProbe.com, n.d. http://www.bibleprobe.com/ backfromthedead.htm.

Pinnock, Clark. "Karl Barth and Christian Apologetics." *Themelios* 2 (1997).

Pytches, David. *Spiritual Gifts in the Local Church.* Minneapolis: Bethany House, 1980.

Rand, William. "What Is Reiki?" The International Center for Reiki Training, n.d. http://www.reiki.org/faq/whatisreiki.html.

Reid, Michael. *Strategic Level Spiritual Warfare: A Modern Mythology? A Detailed Evaluation of the Biblical, Theological and Historical Basis of Spiritual Warfare in Contemporary Thought.* Brentwood, Essex, UK: Michael Reid Ministries, 2002.

Richardson, Michael. "Lessons from the Revival in Argentina." DMin diss., Fuller Theological Seminary, 1998.

Ruthven, Jon. *On the Cessation of the Charismata: The Protestant Polemic on Postbiblical Miracles.* Tulsa, OK: Word & Spirit Press, 2011.

———. *What's Wrong with Protestant Theology? Tradition vs. Biblical Emphasis.* Tulsa, OK: Word & Spirit Press, 2013.

Rutz, James. *Mega Shift.* Colorado Springs, CO: Empowerment Press, 2005.

Servant, David. "Resurrection from the Dead of Pastor Daniel Ekechukwa: Report One of Four." Shepherd Serve: The Teaching Ministry of David Servant, n.d. http://www.heavensfamily.org/ss/resurrection-from-the-dead-pastor-daniel-ekechukwu.

Sithole, Surprise. Surprise Sithole Testimony, n.d. https://s3.amazonaws.com/GA-Podcast/testimonyPodcast/Episode69_Surprise_Sithole.mp4.

Sjogren, Steve. *The Day I Died.* Grand Rapids, MI: Baker, 2006.

Strawbridge, Gregg. "Karl Barth's Rejection of Natural Theology or an Exegesis of Romans 1:19–20." San Francisco, CA, 1997. http://www.wordmp3.com/files/gs/barth.htm.

"Therapeutic Touch Home Page at Pumpkin Hollow Farm—The Northeast Theosophical Retreat Center." Therapeutic Touch Organization, n.d. http://www.therapeutictouch.org/what-is-it.html.

Thiselton. *Life after Death.* Grand Rapids, MI: Eerdmans, 2012.

Torrey, R. "'Why God Used D. L. Moody.'" In *The D. L. Moody Collections.* Chicago: Moody Press, 1997.

Vander Meer, Erwin. "The Strategic Level Spiritual Warfare Theology of C. Peter Wagner and Its Implications for Christian Mission in Malawi." ThD, University of South Africa, 2008.

Wagner, Peter. *Spiritual Warfare Strategies: Confronting Spiritual Powers.* Shippensburg, PA: Destiny Image, 1996.

————. *Territorial Spirits: Practical Strategies for How to Crush the Enemy through Spiritual Warfare.* Shippensburg, PA: Destiny Image, 2012.

Walvoord, John. *The Revelation of Jesus Christ.* Chicago: Moody Press, 1966.

Weatherhead, Leslie. *Psychology, Religion, and Healing.* Nashville: Abingdon, 1952.

————. *Wounded Spirits.* Nashville: Abingdon, 1962.

Wesley, John. "Note on Rev. 4:2." In *Notes on the Whole Bible*, n.d. www .ccel.org.

Wink, Walter. *Engaging the Powers.* Minneapolis: Augsburg Press, 1992.

————. *The Powers That Be: Theology for a New Millennium.* Minneapolis: Augsburg Press, 1998.

————. *Unmasking the Powers.* Minneapolis: Fortress Press, 1986.

ABOUT THE AUTHOR

D r. Clark began ministering, preaching, and pastoring in 1970. He pastored for thirty years in the following denominations: General Baptist, United Church of Christ, American Baptist, Association of Vineyard Churches, and the Apostolic Network of Global Awakening. He has ministered faithfully from November 20, 1970, to today. In addition, he has been traveling as an itinerate minister since January 20, 1994, when God used him to birth the Toronto Blessing, which is now included in some Christian history books as one of the greatest revivals in the twentieth century.

Dr. Clark received a bachelor of science degree with his major, minor, and all electives in religious studies from Oakland City University in 1970, a General Baptist institution. He received his master of divinity from the Southern Baptist Theological Seminary in Louisville, Kentucky, a Southern Baptist institution, in 1977. He received special training from John Wimber in 1994–1996, during which time he planted two Vineyard churches, the first in Illinois, and the second in Missouri. Dr. Clark received his doctor of ministry from United Theological Seminary, a United Methodist institution, in 2013. His doctoral thesis is "A Study of the Effects of Christian Prayer on Pain or Mobility Restrictions from Surgeries Involving Implanted Materials."

During his time at the seminary, Dr. Clark started the Randy

Clark Scholars, a group that had to be approved by Randy to enter into a special doctoral area of study that dealt with the area of discipleship that necessitated embracing the gifts of the Spirit, including the sign gifts, healing, miracles, words of knowledge, prophecy, tongues, and interpretation. Between 2011 and 2017, seventy-two students have participated in the program. Dr. Clark, with the assistance of some of the other Randy Clark Scholars, offers special courses at the Regent Divinity School in Virginia, United Theological Seminary, and Global Awakening Theological Seminary. These courses specialize in physical and emotional healing. He also developed a course that deals with the demonic for the seminaries.

Dr. Clark has written forty-three books, training manuals, workbooks, and small-group course materials, and has created many other products that are audio or visual. He has also created two online training programs certified by the Apostolic Network of Global Awakening and accredited by United Theological Seminary, as well as Regent Divinity School and Global Awakening Theological Seminary. The courses are part of two certification programs: the Christian Healing Certification Program, with tracks in physical healing, inner healing, and deliverance, each with a four-week course; and the Christian Prophecy Certification Program, which consists of five courses. In the first three years, more than two thousand students took 5,690-plus courses.

Dr. Clark not only serves as the founder and president of Global Awakening and the Apostolic Network of Global Awakening, the president of the two certification programs, and as adjunct professor at Regent and United Theological seminaries; he has also established a new seminary fully accredited by the U.S. Department of Education.

Dr. Clark was raised in southern Illinois, the first of three children, by Christian parents. He was the first male in his family to attend school past the eighth grade. He has been married to DeAnne

(Davenport) Clark since July 12, 1975, and they have four children: Joshua, Johannah, Josiah, and Jeremiah. All the children are happily married and have worked with their father in ministry for several years, though some are working toward their own fields of labor that may eventually remove them from the ministry of Global Awakening. DeAnne has been a saint to raise the children by herself due to Dr. Clark's travel schedule. Miraculously, all the children have close relationships with each other, love and honor their parents, and live close together. The Clarks look forward to their monthly family days.

Dr. Clark is guilty of bragging on his children and their accomplishments, and his grandchildren, upon whom he dotes. His oldest three all have children, and Dr. Clark is believing for twelve grandchildren.